M000291376

SEVASTOPOL 1942

Von Manstein's triumph

CAMPAIGN • 189

SEVASTOPOL 1942

Von Manstein's triumph

ROBERT FORCZYK   ILLUSTRATED BY HOWARD GERRARD

First published in Great Britain in 2008 by Osprey Publishing,
PO Box 883, Oxford, OX1 9PL, UK
PO Box 3985, New York, NY 10185-3985, USA
Email: info@ospreypublishing.com

Osprey Publishing is part of the Osprey Group.

© 2008 Osprey Publishing Ltd.

All rights reserved. Apart from any fair dealing for the purpose of private
study, research, criticism or review, as permitted under the Copyright,
Designs and Patents Act, 1988, no part of this publication may be
reproduced, stored in a retrieval system, or transmitted in any form
or by any means, electronic, electrical, chemical, mechanical, optical,
photocopying, recording or otherwise, without the prior written
permission of the copyright owner. Inquiries should be addressed to
the Publishers.

A CIP catalogue record for this book is available from the British Library

ISBN: 978 1 84603 221 9

Editorial by Ilios Publishing Ltd, Oxford, UK (www.iliospublishing.com)
Page layout by The Black Spot
Index by Alan Thatcher
Maps by the Map Studio Ltd
3D bird's-eye views by The Black Spot
Battlescene illustrations by Howard Gerrard
Typeset in Myriad Pro and Sabon
Originated by PPS Grasmere Ltd, Leeds, UK
Printed in China through World Print Ltd.

13 14 15 16 17   16 15 14 13 12 11 10 9 8 7

The Woodland Trust
Osprey Publishing is supporting the Woodland Trust, the UK's leading
woodland conservation charity, by funding the dedication of trees.

www.ospreypublishing.com

DEDICATION

This volume is dedicated to Major Douglas A. Zembiec, US Marines,
killed during combat operations near Baghdad, 10 May 2007.

ACKNOWLEDGEMENTS

I wish to thank Nik Cornish, Monika Geilen at the Bundesarchiv,
Peter Harrington (curator of the Anne S. K. Brown collection at Brown
University), Ted Nevill of TRH Pictures, HITM Photo Archives and the
staff at the National Archives and Research Administration (NARA)
for their assistance in assembling photographs for this volume.

ARTIST'S NOTE

Readers may care to note that the original paintings from which the
battlescene colour plates in this book were prepared is available for
private sale. All reproduction copyright whatsoever is retained by
the Publishers. All enquiries should be addressed to:

Howard Gerrard
11 Oaks Road
Tenterden
Kent
TN30 6RD

The Publishers regret that they can enter into no correspondence
upon this matter.

Key to military symbols

CONTENTS

ORIGINS OF THE CAMPAIGN

The original *Barbarossa* plans in 1941 had not even addressed Sevastopol or the Crimea since it was assumed that, once the main Soviet forces were annihilated west of the Dnepr River, peripheral areas such as the Crimea would fall in the subsequent mop-up operations. Sevastopol and the Soviet Black Sea Fleet were not expected to have any influence on German ground operations in the Ukraine. However, on 13 July 1941, six DB-3 naval bombers from the Black Sea Fleet's air arm (Voyenno-Vozdushnye Sily – Chernomorskiy Flot) attacked oil refineries outside Ploesti and set 9,000 tons of oil on fire and left one refinery burning for three days. Five days later, another attack destroyed 2,000 more tons of oil. Although these attacks were small, the amount of fuel destroyed was enough to provide five loads of fuel for every Panzer division in the USSR, so Hitler was duly alarmed. While his characterization of Sevastopol as an 'unsinkable aircraft carrier' was exaggerated, small-scale air raids against Axis oil supplies did indicate a potential vulnerability that needed to be addressed.

In reaction to these Soviet air raids, an addendum to Führer Directive 33 was issued on 23 July 1941, in which the Oberkommando der Wehrmacht (OKW) stipulated that 'the capture of the Ukraine, the Crimea and the territory of the Russian Federation to the Don' was now a 'priority mission'. On 12 August 1941, the OKW clarified the specified mission for Army Group

German infantry in pursuit of the defeated Soviets after the breakthrough at Ishun on 30 October 1941. In two days, the spearheads of Eleventh Army marched over 100km and captured the capital of the Crimea, Simferopol. (Nik Cornish Archive, WH336)

Strategic dispositions, 24 September 1941–7 May 1942

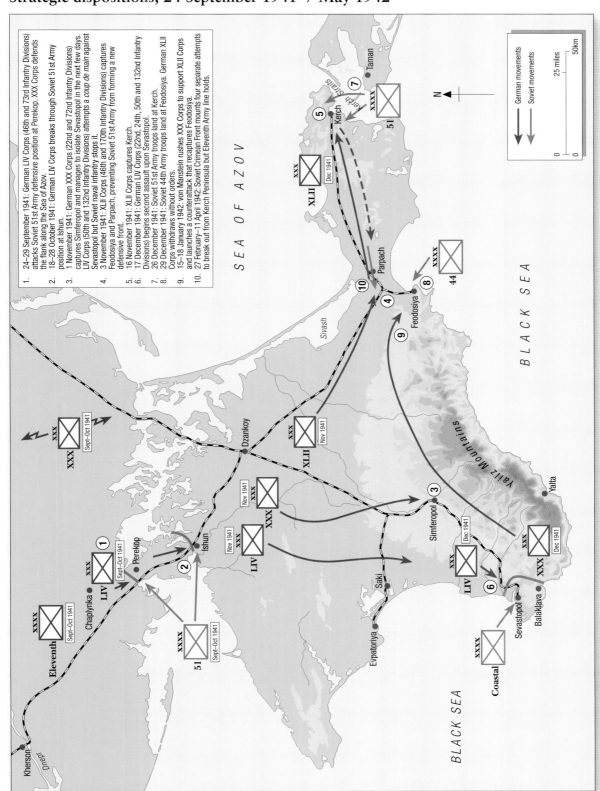

1. 24–29 September 1941: German LIV Corps (46th and 73rd Infantry Divisions) attacks Soviet 51st Army defensive position at Perekop. XXX Corps defends the flank along the Sea of Azov.
2. 18–28 October 1941: German LIV Corps breaks through Soviet 51st Army position at Ishun.
3. 1 November 1941: German XXX Corps (22nd and 72nd Infantry Divisions) captures Simferopol and manages to isolate Sevastopol in the next few days. LIV Corps (50th and 132nd Infantry Divisions) attempts a *coup de main* against Sevastopol but Soviet naval infantry stops it.
4. 3 November 1941: XLII Corps (46th and 170th Infantry Divisions) captures Feodosiya and Parpach, preventing Soviet 51st Army from forming a new defensive front.
5. 16 November 1941: XLII Corps captures Kerch.
6. 17 December 1941: German LIV Corps (22nd, 24th, 50th and 132nd Infantry Divisions) begins second assault upon Sevastopol.
7. 26 December 1941: Soviet 51st Army troops land at Kerch.
8. 29 December 1941: Soviet 44th Army troops land at Feodosiya. German XLII Corps withdraws without orders.
9. 15–18 January 1942: von Manstein rushes XXX Corps to support XLII Corps and launches a counterattack that recaptures Feodosiya.
10. 27 February–11 April 1942: Soviet Crimean Front mounts four separate attempts to break out from Kerch Peninsula but Eleventh Army line holds.

7

An Axis motorized column advances toward Sevastopol. Von Manstein formed a mobile *Kampfgruppe*, composed of motorized anti-aircraft and *Panzerjäger* units as well as a Romanian motorized infantry regiment, to try and reach the port before Soviet reinforcements arrived. (Nik Cornish Archive, WH712)

South by stating that, 'the capture of the Crimea, which being an enemy air base, poses an especially great threat to the Romanian oilfields' and that the Crimea would be used as a springboard to cross the Kerch Straits into the Caucasus. Hitler apparently didn't think that the OKW directive went far enough and on 21 August 1941 he ordered that, 'the most important missions before the onset of winter are to seize the Crimea and the industrial and coal regions of the Don …' and that, 'the seizure of the Crimean Peninsula has colossal importance for the protection of oil supplies from Romania'. Thus, the German rationale for conquering the Crimea was initially based upon the need to protect their own oil supplies and to facilitate projecting German ground power toward Soviet oil sources in the Caucasus.

Generaloberst Erich von Manstein took command of the Eleventh Army on 17 September 1941, just as that formation was in the process of crossing the Dnepr River at Berislav. The Oberkommando des Heeres (OKH) had tasked the Eleventh Army with two diverging missions: the pursuit of retreating Soviet forces eastwards toward Rostov and the conquest of the Crimea. Von Manstein realized that he had insufficient forces to accomplish both missions simultaneously so he gave priority to the Crimea. Only a week after taking command, von Manstein launched General der Kavallerie Erik Hansen's LIV Corps (45th and 73rd Infantry Divisions) into a furious assault upon the Soviet position at the Perekop Isthmus, which guarded the entrance to the Crimea. After six days of heavy fighting and suffering 2,641 casualties, LIV Corps was finally able to break through and scatter the Soviet defenders but in the meantime, the Soviet Southern Front launched a major counteroffensive against Eleventh Army's thinly held front around Melitopol. Von Manstein was forced to break off the attack on the Crimea and to commit his reserves to defeat the Soviet counteroffensive, which resulted in the destruction of the bulk of two Soviet armies (see Campaign 129: *Operation Barbarossa 1941 (1) Army Group South* Osprey Publishing Ltd: Oxford, 2003).

By October 1941, the OKH realized that the Eleventh Army could not accomplish both missions and gave the task of pursuit eastwards to von Kleist's 1st Panzergruppe, while von Manstein was ordered to resume his offensive in the Crimea. Meanwhile, the Soviet Stavka had been able to rush reinforcements to the Crimea and re-establish a front farther south at Ishun.

The Soviets quickly raised six battalions of naval infantry from ships' crews at Sevastopol in early November 1941 in order to fend off the approaching German divisions. This group of naval infantry are a mixed group from the heavy cruiser *Krasny Kavkaz* and the destroyer *Smyshlonnyi*. (Author's collection)

Once again, von Manstein ordered Hansen's LIV Corps (22nd, 46th and 73rd Infantry Divisions) to conduct a deliberate frontal assault in a narrow sector against prepared defences. The defending Soviet 51st Army at Ishun was superior in numbers and had armour reserves, as well as local air superiority. Despite these disadvantages, Hansen's corps slowly chewed its way through the Soviet defensive lines in a succession of attacks between 18 and 28 October. The arrival of three groups of Bf 109 fighters was instrumental in breaking the Soviet air superiority over Ishun. In 12 days of heavy fighting, LIV Corps suffered approximately 5,376 casualties, but Soviet losses were much higher. By the end of October, 51st Army's front had been pierced and it was in full retreat toward the interior of the Crimea.

Once a breakthrough at Ishun was achieved, von Manstein switched to pursuit and his infantry force-marched quickly to seize the capital of the Crimea – Simferopol – on 1 November. Some of the defeated Soviet troops were able to reach safety at Sevastopol, but the rest were lost when Kerch fell on 16 November. Sevastopol was the only Soviet foothold left in the Crimea. Von Manstein's conquest of most of the Crimea in less than a month was a tremendous achievement, particularly considering the supply difficulties and adverse terrain. However, the German triumph in the Crimea was incomplete as long as fortress Sevastopol was still in Soviet hands and von Manstein resolved to eliminate this final enclave as quickly as possible. The Soviet Stavka was equally resolved to hold onto Sevastopol as a springboard for future offensives and quickly directed reinforcements toward the city.

THE SIEGE BEGINS, 30 OCTOBER–9 NOVEMBER 1941

When the 51st Army front at Ishun collapsed, Vice-Admiral Oktyabrsky put the naval base on alert and assumed command of the Sevastopol Defence Region – Sevastopolskogo Oboronitelnogo Raiona (SOR) – on 4 November 1941. The city of Sevastopol had a population of 111,000 in 1941 and Oktyabrsky drafted thousands of them to complete quickly three defensive belts around the city before the Germans arrived. However, there were very few troops available to defend the base, only the 7th Naval Infantry Brigade

The German offensive, 17–26 December 1941

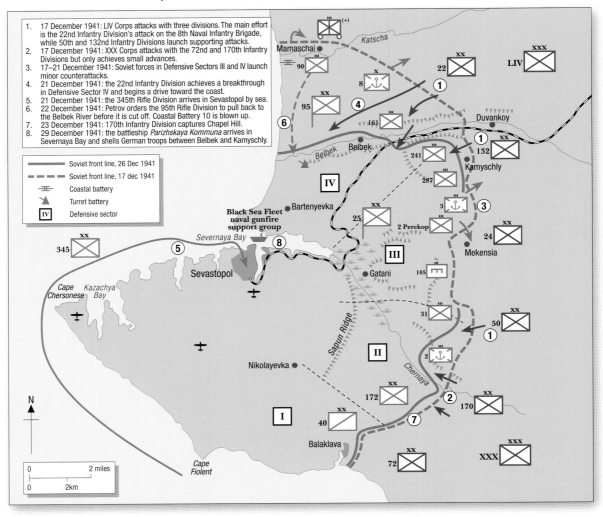

1. 17 December 1941: LIV Corps attacks with three divisions. The main effort is the 22nd Infantry Division's attack on the 8th Naval Infantry Brigade, while 50th and 132nd Infantry Divisions launch supporting attacks.
2. 17 December 1941: XXX Corps attacks with the 72nd and 170th Infantry Divisions but only achieves small advances.
3. 17–21 December 1941: Soviet forces in Defensive Sectors III and IV launch minor counterattacks.
4. 21 December 1941: the 22nd Infantry Division achieves a breakthrough in Defensive Sector IV and begins a drive toward the coast.
5. 21 December 1941: the 345th Rifle Division arrives in Sevastopol by sea.
6. 22 December 1941: Petrov orders the 95th Rifle Division to pull back to the Belbek River before it is cut off. Coastal Battery 10 is blown up.
7. 23 December 1941: 170th Infantry Division captures Chapel Hill.
8. 29 December 1941: the battleship *Parizhskaya Kommuna* arrives in Severnaya Bay and shells German troops between Belbek and Kamyschly.

Soviet front line, 26 Dec 1941
Soviet front line, 17 dec 1941
Coastal battery
Turret battery
Defensive sector

(5,200 men), two battalions of sailors, two battalions of naval cadets and the 61st Anti-Aircraft Artillery Regiment. The Black Sea Fleet quickly brought in the 8th Naval Infantry Brigade from Novorossiysk on 30 October and four more naval infantry battalions were formed from ship crews. Oktyabrsky deployed the 8th Naval Infantry Brigade to defend the north-east sector, while the 7th Naval Infantry Brigade held the centre around Mekenzyya Village. Only construction units held the flanks around Mamaschai and Balaklava. With fewer than 20,000 troops to defend the base, Oktyabrsky decided to rely heavily upon General-Major Morgunov's 12 batteries of coastal artillery and naval gunfire to slow down the German advance upon the port, buying time until reinforcements could arrive. Although weak on the ground, the initial Soviet defence also enjoyed near-complete air superiority, with the 62nd Fighter Brigade's 61 operational fighters dominating the skies around the city.

Sevastopol's defenders were still trying to throw together a cohesive defence when forward observers detected the spearhead of the German 132nd Infantry Division, advancing south along the Black Sea coast on 30 October. Outside Simferopol, Kampfgruppe Ziegler came under long-range fire from the 305mm guns of Sevastopol's Coastal Battery 30 (soon to be known as Fort Maxim Gorky I to the Germans) at 1230hrs on 1 November.

Von Manstein had hoped to seize Sevastopol in a *coup de main* but he lacked the mobile forces, artillery and air support to make a quick dash for the city. Instead, Von Manstein ordered Hansen to push the 132nd Infantry Division down the Simferopol–Sevastopol railway line toward the Belbek River Valley while Fretter-Pico's 72nd Infantry Division detoured through the mountains to Yalta and then approached Sevastopol from the east. The 132nd Infantry Division advanced fairly rapidly down the railway line, brushing aside a battalion of naval cadets sent to delay them and reached the railway bridge over the Belbek River by nightfall on 2 November. However, the German *Landser* soon ran into the 8th Naval Infantry Brigade west of Duvankoy and the pursuit ground to a halt; the 132nd Infantry Division suffered 428 casualties on 2–3 November. For the next week, von Manstein was unable to advance and hurriedly tried to bring up more divisions for a coordinated attack.

With the German advance stymied by only two brigades of naval infantry, Oktyabrsky used his fleet to bring in 23,000 more reinforcements from the Caucasus. On 9 November, General-Major Ivan Petrov's Coastal Army reached Balaklava from Yalta, bringing 19,894 troops, ten T-26 light tanks, 152 guns and 200 mortars. Oktyabrsky then had about 52,000 troops available to defend the city. Although the Luftwaffe was still relatively weak in the Crimea, the Fleet's Military Council decided that only a naval gunfire support unit consisting of the heavy cruiser *Krasny Kavkaz*, light cruisers *Krasny Krym* and *Chervona Ukraina*, and seven destroyers should remain to protect the port.

THE GERMAN ASSAULT: 10–21 NOVEMBER 1941

Von Manstein wanted to launch an immediate assault upon Sevastopol before the end of November, but his supply situation was awful. Lacking heavy artillery or effective air support, he decided to avoid the main Soviet defensive positions around the Belbek River Valley and to probe for weak spots in the centre of their line. On 10 November, the 50th Infantry Division began advancing towards the lower Chernaya River and captured Uppa and the next day the 132nd Infantry Division attacked and captured the village of Mekenzyya, only 4km east of Severnaya Bay. However, Petrov was able to move up the 2nd Naval Infantry Regiment and the 172nd Rifle Division to block any further German advance in this sector. Oktyabrsky used his naval gunfire group, coastal artillery and air group to wear down von Manstein's small assault groups.

Fretter-Pico approached Balaklava from the east with the 72nd Infantry Division by 15 November, but Oktyabrsky sent the battleship *Parizhskaya Kommuna* and two light cruisers to bombard this flank attack. Von Manstein reinforced Hansen with the 22nd Infantry Division, enabling a renewed attack with three divisions in the centre while 72nd Infantry Division probed in the south. However, this weak offensive made virtually no progress and ground to a halt as Petrov committed his reserves. Von Manstein called off the offensive on 21 November, after the Eleventh Army had suffered nearly 2,000 casualties. Frustrated by his inability to push his way into Sevastopol with a series of hasty attacks, von Manstein now realized that he would have to organize a deliberate offensive in order to overcome the increasingly formidable defences.

THE GERMAN ASSAULT: 17 DECEMBER 1941

After the suspension of all the other Axis offensives on the Eastern Front in December 1941, von Manstein found himself the only German commander who was still vested with an offensive mission. Hitler hoped that the capture of fortress Sevastopol would partly offset the failure of Operation *Typhoon* to capture Moscow and boost German morale on the home front. Von Manstein was ordered to capture Sevastopol by the end of the year with the forces he had available.

Oktyabrsky used the interval between the first and second German offensives to bring in additional reinforcements and to strengthen his defences. The Black Sea Fleet transported 11,000 troops of the newly formed 388th Rifle Division into Sevastopol on 7–13 December and replacements allowed Petrov to rebuild some of his battle-weary formations. Soviet engineers began to lay extensive minefields and barbed wire belts around key defensive positions. By mid-December, Petrov had a fairly strong defensive perimeter, although the naval commanders demanded that he hold the area north of the Belbek River in order to retain Coastal Battery 10 near Mamaschai.

Von Manstein made Hansen's LIV Corps the main effort for the December offensive, since XXX Corps had only two divisions in the Balaklava sector by mid-December. The LIV Corps was down to a combat strength of only 15,551 men in its four tired infantry divisions (22nd, 24th, 50th and 132nd). Over 7,000 troops in Eleventh Army were on the sick list by late December and no infantry reserves were available. Nor did the Eleventh Army have much heavy artillery and it was desperately short of artillery ammunition. Furthermore, in order to mass Eleventh Army for the offensive, von Manstein had to accept great risk, leaving the weak XLII Corps with the 46th Infantry Division and two Romanian brigades to guard the entire Crimean coastline from Yalta to Kerch.

The German offensive began at 0610hrs on 17 December 1941, with a concentrated artillery bombardment. Fliegerkorps VIII had returned to the Crimea and air strikes from 34 Ju 87 Stukas and 20 bombers hit the Soviet forward positions. Hansen's LIV Corps attacked with the 22nd Infantry

The light cruiser *Krasny Krym* under attack from Stukas on 12 November 1941. This ship was ordered to stay behind as part of a small naval gunfire support group that provided artillery fire for the hard-pressed defenders in November– December 1941. During 1942, *Krasny Krym* made repeated runs into Sevastopol, carrying in troops and evacuating wounded back to Novorossiysk. (Author's collection)

Division against the 8th Naval Infantry Brigade north of the Belbek River, while the 50th and 132nd Infantry Divisions conducted fixing attacks against the Soviet centre. Oktyabrsky's decision to defend north of the Belbek River was now revealed as an over-extension, as the 22nd Infantry Division rolled up the right flank of the 8th Naval Infantry Brigade and began to push a wedge toward the coast. After five days of costly fighting, Petrov finally abandoned the Mamaschai salient and withdrew the battered 8th Naval Infantry Brigade and the 90th Rifle Regiment to the north bank of the Belbek Valley. Meanwhile in the south, XXX Corps attacked with the 72nd and 170th Infantry Divisions and was able to push the 172nd Rifle Division back in some places, but they could not achieve a breakthrough. The only real success was achieved on 23 December, when the 170th Infantry Division and the Romanian 1st Mountain Brigade captured Chapel Hill, a key position in Sevastopol's Defensive Sector II.

Aided by Soviet naval supremacy and the long winter nights, Vice-Admiral Oktyabrsky was able to bring in the 79th Naval Infantry Brigade and the 345th Rifle Division to strengthen the Soviet ground defences. Meanwhile, the battleship *Parizhskaya Kommuna* and its naval gunfire group played a critical role, moving in to shell the German forward infantry wherever a breakthrough threatened. Nor did the Soviets intend to remain meekly on the defensive. While von Manstein had the bulk of Eleventh Army tied down around Sevastopol, the Soviets decided to use their naval superiority to attack the weakly held eastern side of the Crimea.

Supported by the Azov Flotilla, the Soviet 51st Army under General-Lieutenant Lvov landed almost 5,000 troops near Kerch on the morning of 26 December. The initial landings were poorly executed and von Manstein thought that the 46th Infantry Division alone could contain them. However, the Soviet Black Sea Fleet seized the port of Feodosiya in a bold *coup de main* on 29 December and landed 23,000 troops and a battalion of tanks from the 44th Army. Realizing that it was about to be cut off, XLII Corps withdrew without orders to the Parpach narrows. The successful Soviet landing forced von Manstein to call off the attack on Sevastopol. He shifted XXX Corps from Sevastopol to reinforce XLII Corps and re-establish a new line near Feodosiya, effectively sealing the Soviet 44th and 51st Armies in the Kerch Peninsula. The Soviet amphibious landings – their largest of the war – succeeded in seizing the initiative in the Crimea and saving Sevastopol.

ABOVE

German troops constructing defensive positions outside Sevastopol in December 1941. After the initial attempts to storm the city failed, the Eleventh Army settled in for a long siege. By Christmas, over 7,000 German troops were on the sick list. (HITM Photo Research)

ABOVE LEFT

A battery of 10cm s.K 18 guns from the 818th Artillery Battalion receiving counterbattery fire during the offensive in December 1941. Von Manstein had only eight of these long-range guns available and they were a high-priority target for the Soviet coastal batteries and naval gunfire. (HITM Photo Research)

After Soviet naval landings near Feodosiya, Kerch and Evpatoria in the winter of 1941–42 the Germans had to constantly watch the Crimean coastline for signs of new Soviet invasions. Here, a German soldier with an MG08 adapted for anti-aircraft duty, watches a section of the southern Crimean coastline in April 1942. (HITM Photo Research)

The German December offensive at Sevastopol had failed, and the two attacking German corps suffered 8,595 casualties between 17 and 31 December. Soviet losses during the fighting in November–December 1941 were also serious, including over 7,000 killed and 20,000 captured. Nevertheless, von Manstein was unwilling to cede the initiative to the enemy and he organized a hasty counterattack on 15 January that recaptured Feodosiya. However, the Eleventh Army lacked the strength to finish off the Soviet 44th and 51st Armies in the Kerch Peninsula and the Stavka reinforced this front with nine rifle divisions.

Stalin ordered the newly formed Crimean Front under General-Lieutenant Dmitri T. Kozlov to break out from this bridgehead and liberate the entire Crimea. Kozlov launched a series of offensives in February, March and April that were all repulsed with heavy losses. Petrov's Coastal Army also launched an attack against Hansen's LIV Corps on 26 February 1942 that inflicted over 1,200 casualties on the besiegers, but at the cost of more than 2,500 Soviet losses. As the spring thaw arrived in the Crimea, both sides prepared for offensive action to decide the campaign. Fortress Sevastopol stood defiant, succoured by the Black Sea Fleet and with much improved defences over the winter. The German position in the Crimea appeared unpromising, with a large enemy force at one end of the peninsula and a virtually impregnable fortress at the other end.

CHRONOLOGY

1941

22 June   The Luftwaffe begins mine-laying operations around Sevastopol.

24–28 September   German Eleventh Army attacks the Soviet defences at the Perekop Isthmus.

15 October   Soviets abandon Odessa and evacuate Coastal Army to Sevastopol.

18–28 October   Eleventh Army achieves a breakthrough at Perekop and Germans begin pursuit into the Crimea.

30 October   Siege of Sevastopol begins when Soviet batteries fire on approaching German troops.

2–3 November   German attempt to seize Sevastopol in a *coup de main* fails.

4 November   Vice-Admiral Oktyabrsky assumes command of the Sevastopol Defence District (SOR).

9 November   Independent Coastal Army reaches Sevastopol.

10–21 November   First German offensive at Sevastopol fails.

15 November   XLII Corps captures Kerch.

17–22 December   Eleventh Army begins second offensive at Sevastopol. After five days of fighting, Soviets are forced to pull back to the Belbek Valley.

26–29 December   Soviet 51st Army lands at Kerch and 44th Army at Feodosiya.

30 December   Eleventh Army calls off the offensive at Sevastopol, sending XXX Corps to deal with Soviet amphibious landings.

1942

15–18 January   Eleventh Army recaptures Feodosiya.

26 February– 5 March   While Soviet armies attempt to break out of the Kerch Peninsula, the Coastal Army attacks LIV Corps at Sevastopol. All Soviet attacks fail with heavy losses.

13 March– 11 April   Three more Soviet attempts to break out from Kerch fail.

8 May   Eleventh Army begins Operation *Trappenjagd*.

15 May   German 170th Infantry Division enters Kerch.

15–20 May   Soviet 51st and 44th Armies evacuate survivors from Kerch Peninsula.

2 June   German Eleventh Army begins five-day artillery and air attack preparation on Sevastopol.

5 June	'Dora' begins firing at Sevastopol.	XXX Corps overruns most of the Fedyukhiny Heights.
6 June	German artillery fire knocks out one gun turret at Fort Maxim Gorky I.	
		22 June	German LIV Corps launches major attack with two divisions against the Soviet Defensive Sector III.
7 June	The German LIV Corps launches the main ground attack with four divisions across the Kamyschly Ravine against the Soviet Defensive Sector III.	
		23 June	Von Richthofen departs. Fort Konstantinovsky falls, last Soviet position on north side of Severnaya Bay.
9 June	German 22nd Infantry Division captures the Mekenziyevy Mountain train station.	
		24 June	Romanian Mountain Corps launches major attack toward Bastion II.
11 June	Soviet counterattack to retake the Forsthaus fails. XXX Corps seizes Ruin Hill.	25 June	Romanians capture Bastion II.
		26 June	142nd Naval Rifle Brigade arrives in Sevastopol.
12 June	XXX Corps seizes Kamary.	
13 June	Fort Stalin captured by German 22nd Infantry Division. The Soviet 138th Naval Infantry Brigade arrives in Sevastopol.	28 June	Last resupply convoy enters Sevastopol.
		29 June	The German LIV Corps conducts an assault crossing of Severnaya Bay, while the 50th and 132nd Infantry Divisions attack toward Inkerman. Simultaneously, XXX Corps captures Sapun Ridge and advances to the English Cemetery.
17 June	LIV Corps launches a major attack with four divisions that achieves a breakthrough in the Soviet Defensive Sector IV. Fort Maxim Gorky I is overrun, with the garrison trapped inside. Soviet forts GPU, Tscheka, Molotov and Volga are captured.	
		30 June	The Soviet Stavka orders senior cadre to evacuate Sevastopol. Novikov abandons Balaklava and withdraws his forces to the Chersonese Peninsula.
17 June	Romanian 1st Mountain Division captures Sugar Loaf Hill.	
18 June	German reconnaissance troops capture the Eagle's Perch. Bartenyevka falls to 24th Infantry Division.	1 July	General-Major Petrov and his staff leave by submarine. Vice-Admiral Oktyabrsky and staff are flown out. German LIV Corps and Romanians advance into ruins of Sevastopol. Hitler promotes von Manstein to Generalfeldmarschall.
19 June	German 132nd Infantry Division captures Coastal Battery 12.	
20 June	Fort Lenin is captured, North Fort under attack.	2 July	Garrison blows up Coastal Battery 35.
21 June	North Fort surrenders. Petrov orders evacuation of all Soviet positions on north side of Severnaya Bay.	4 July	Cape Chersonese airstrip is captured and last organized Soviet resistance ends.

OPPOSING PLANS

GERMAN PLANS

Once the Soviet winter counteroffensives came to a close, the OKW issued Führer Directive 41 on 5 April 1942, which declared that 'mopping up operations in the Kerch Peninsula and the capture of Sevastopol' were merely preliminary operations before the main thrust by Army Group South in *Fall Blau* began on 28 June. When von Manstein met with Hitler in the Wolfsschanze (Wolf's Lair) in East Prussia in mid-April 1942 to brief him on plans for the Crimea, Hitler quickly approved his concept for the attack on Sevastopol but told him that Fliegerkorps VIII would be withdrawn even before the end of the assault. Hitler was not particularly interested in Sevastopol by this point in the war, his focus having shifted to the upcoming summer offensive. Von Manstein was also directed to begin preparations for crossing the Kerch Straits immediately after the fall of Sevastopol and to conduct the operation no later than mid-August 1942.

Von Manstein's plan for conquering Sevastopol had evolved from his relatively simple jabs in the fall of 1941, which had failed to collapse the hastily erected Soviet defences. By May 1942, von Manstein knew that Sevastopol would be a hard nut to crack and he prepared for a deliberate and sustained assault that could gradually rip through its defences. The offensive, named Operation *Störfang* (Sturgeon Haul) would be assisted by a massive superiority in artillery and air support. Unlike a typical German campaign based upon manoeuvre, *Störfang* was based upon firepower. However, von Manstein's plan was threatened by shortages of ammunition and infantry reserves, as well as by a rigid time schedule; he had to win quickly and he could not call upon the rest of Army Group South for assistance if the attack bogged down. Thus, in order to fulfil his orders von Manstein would have to husband his

Hitler promised von Manstein that he would receive the 800mm railway gun 'Dora' for the final assault on Sevastopol. This immense weapon weighed 1,328 tons and required days of engineer work to both assemble the weapon and construct a firing position near Bakhchysaray. Even though 'Dora' was specifically designed to crack open armoured forts, during Operation *Störfang* the weapon was misused against a variety of secondary targets and failed to destroy the armoured Coastal Batteries 30 and 35. (Anne S. K. Brown)

RIGHT
The Bolsheviks will be driven off and never return!' proclaims a propaganda poster distributed by the Eleventh Army in the Crimea. This poster ties in with von Manstein's secret memorandum about annihilating the 'Judaeo-Bolshevik' system and depicts the Wehrmacht acting as exterminators under the Nazi banner. (NARA)

FAR RIGHT
'Black Sea Sailors! Not a step back! Beat the Fascists at Sevastopol!' proclaims a Soviet propaganda poster. Communist propaganda preferred using sailors to rally patriotic sentiment, since they were closely associated with the Bolshevik Revolution of 1917. (Author's collection)

resources to avoid heavy losses, but also make rapid progress and emerge with Eleventh Army capable of immediately engaging in a challenging follow-on mission. It was a tall order for any commander or any army.

Von Manstein intended Hansen's LIV Corps to make the main effort in the north with a very strong breakthrough attack, while Fretter-Pico's weaker XXX Corps would mount a supporting attack to tie down Soviet reserves. Little offensive role was envisaged for the Romanian Mountain Corps, which was merely intended to hold the centre between the two German corps, although von Manstein would draw upon their infantry and artillery and transfer it to German command as needed.

SOVIET PLANS

The Soviets had begun constructing an inner defensive line extending out 5–8km from Sevastopol on 4 July 1941, as well as planning a main defensive line extending out to 10km from the city and a forward line extending out even farther. Some barbed wire and mines were emplaced in August but the two outer lines were still incomplete when German forces began approaching the city in October 1941. The SOR was divided into four defensive sectors. The two sectors most likely to be attacked by the enemy were Defensive Sector IV, which covered the Belbek River Valley and the western coast, and Defensive Sector III, which covered the hilly area between Kamyschly and Mekenzyya Village; both of these sectors had a front-line length of 8.5km. Defensive Sector II covered the Chernaya River Valley and the approaches to the vital Sapun Heights; this sector was the widest with a front-line length of 12km. Defensive Sector I, which was only 7.5km long, was extremely well fortified and covered the mountainous terrain between Rose Hill and Balaklava. Each sector was commanded by one of the division commanders, but the naval coastal batteries in Defensive Sectors I and IV remained under the direction of General-Major Petr Morgunov, commander of Sevastopol's coastal defences.

A German leaders' reconnaissance from the 72nd Infantry Division near Chapel Hill in May 1942. The soldier pointing is probably the company *Hauptfeldwebel* and the company commander is kneeling. (HITM Photo Research)

A Soviet infantry unit in an assembly area near Sevastopol, summer 1942. Note the mix of SVT-40 automatic rifles, Mosin-Nagant bolt-action rifles and PPSh submachine-guns, as well as the presence of several females. This is probably a unit from the 172nd Rifle Division, which had a large contingent of locally raised militia in its ranks. (Central Museum of the Armed Forces, Moscow)

In each defensive sector, Soviet troops had constructed trenches, bunkers, minefields and wire obstacles to supplement the existing coastal defences. Throughout the siege the Soviets continued to improve these fortifications and by May 1942 they had become very formidable. Oktyabrsky and Petrov intended to use their dense obstacle belt to wear down any attacking German infantry in an attritional battle, a formula that they had employed with great success against the Romanians at Odessa in 1941. As long as the Black Sea Fleet could keep delivering infantry replacements to keep the ground defence viable, this plan had good chances of success. In time, the Germans would weary and stop, as they had in November and December

A well-camouflaged Soviet earth and timber gun bunker at Sevastopol. Inside this position, a 76mm gun was protected by up to 2m of timber and stone. Over 3,000 bunkers protected Sevastopol. (Nik Cornish Archive, WH98)

A German Ju 87 Stuka pilot prepares for take-off. German plans for the capture of Sevastopol were premised upon the commitment of overwhelming air support and von Manstein's Eleventh Army would receive direct support from two Stuka *Gruppen* for the offensive. (Nik Cornish Archive, WH407)

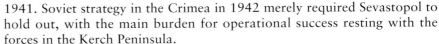

1941. Soviet strategy in the Crimea in 1942 merely required Sevastopol to hold out, with the main burden for operational success resting with the forces in the Kerch Peninsula.

However, the Stavka's plans for the Crimea were undermined by a dangerous under-estimation of German capabilities in the area and an exaggerated sense of Sevastopol's impregnability. The Stavka did not expect any major Axis reinforcements for the Crimea in spring 1942 and were particularly dismissive of the effects of Luftwaffe air superiority over Sevastopol. Too much Soviet effort went into sustaining the Kerch lodgement with the result that Sevastopol's defenders did not have adequate ammunition or reserves for a protracted battle. Oktyabrsky and Petrov based their defensive plans on two ultimately false assumptions – that any renewed German assault would last for no more than ten days and that the garrison could count upon a Soviet offensive from the Kerch Peninsula to draw off von Manstein's reserves.

OPPOSING LEADERS

GERMAN

Generaloberst Erich von Manstein (1887–1973), commander of the Eleventh Army. Von Manstein came from a Prussian military family and was a nephew of General Paul von Hindenburg. During World War I, von Manstein served primarily as a staff officer after being badly wounded in Poland in November 1914. In the interwar period, von Manstein rose rapidly in the General Staff hierarchy and at the start of World War II he was chief of staff of von Rundstedt's Army Group South in Poland and then Army Group A on the Western Front. It was von Manstein's proposals that resulted in the *Sichelschnitt* plan that resulted in a quick and decisive victory over France in 1940. At the outset of Operation *Barbarossa*, von Manstein commanded LVI Panzer Corps in Army Group North, which quickly advanced across Lithuania to seize crossings over the Dvina River.

There is no doubt that von Manstein possessed operational talent, but he lacked the 'feel' for the common soldier that commanders like Rommel or Guderian possessed. He much preferred spending time in his captured castle on the Black Sea coast near Yalta to visiting front-line trenches. His treatment of his subordinates and the Romanians throughout *Störfang* was rather shabby.

Generaloberst Erich von Manstein, commander of the Eleventh Army. Von Manstein was a talented commander but he rarely visited the front lines and photos such as these were intended more for propaganda value than to convey his typical routine. In fact, von Manstein spent much of the siege of Sevastopol at his comfortable requisitioned castle on the Black Sea coast. (Nik Cornish Archive, WH722)

RIGHT
General der Artillerie Maximilian Fretter-Pico, commander of XXX Corps. Fretter-Pico had spent most of the first two years of the war in staff assignments and had gained only limited command experience before being given a corps. He was a rather unimaginative, set-piece commander. (Bundesarchiv, 146-1992-44-36A)

FAR RIGHT
General der Kavallerie Erik Hansen, commander of LIV Corps. Hansen had gained considerable experience as a division commander in 1939–40 and as a corps commander he became adept at conducting breakthrough attacks. Von Manstein valued Hansen for his aggressiveness and 'can-do' attitude. (Bundesarchiv, 89-BP24/5/)

After the war, von Manstein was able to shape successfully the historiography of his role in the war by portraying himself as a 'great captain'. However, he also sought to conceal the fact that he was intimately involved in the wartime atrocities of the Third Reich. There is no mention in von Manstein's memoir about his secret order issued on 20 November 1941 entitled, 'the Annihilation of the Judaeo-Bolshevik system'. This order, signed by von Manstein himself, said that Jews were 'instigators of all disorders' in the rear areas and said that, 'the soldier should understand the necessity of punishment of Jewry'. Nor does von Manstein's memoir mention his collaboration with the genocidal activities of SS-Einsatzgruppe D that followed the Eleventh Army into the Crimea. Yet the SS Commander of that unit testified after the war that, 'in Simferopol the [Eleventh] army command requested the *Einsatzkommandos* in its area hasten liquidations because famine was threatening and there was a great housing shortage'. The SS duly murdered 14,300 civilians in Simferopol on 13 December 1941 – at a time when von Manstein's headquarters was located in the same town. The former SS commander also stated that von Manstein's staff demanded that the wristwatches from murdered civilians be sent to the Eleventh Army, since the troops in the front lines needed them. After the fall of Sevastopol, von Manstein allowed the SS a free hand in murdering both civilians and captured prisoners in Sevastopol. As a commander, von Manstein certainly demonstrated that he was capable of conducting bold and efficient operations, but he was also actively involved in Nazi atrocities in the Soviet Union. Unlike a true 'great captain', such as Erwin Rommel, von Manstein neither treated his subordinates with loyalty, his vanquished enemies with a sense of chivalry or his political master with the contempt that he deserved.

General der Artillerie Maximilian Fretter-Pico (1892–1984) was commander of XXX Corps from 27 December 1941 to 16 July 1944. Fretter-Pico had an undistinguished career as a junior staff officer in World War I and he missed the Polish campaign and the bulk of the French campaign. At the start of *Barbarossa*, Fretter-Pico was given his first command assignment, the 97th Jäger Division in Army Group South. After eight months of divisional

FAR LEFT
Generalmajor Ludwig Wolff, commander of the 22nd Infantry Division. Wolff was an early star, winning the Knight's Cross in May 1940 fighting the BEF in Belgium. At Sevastopol, Wolff suffered an eye injury and spent the next two years in training assignments. (Bundesarchiv, 71/48/9)

LEFT
Oberst Dietrich von Choltitz, commander of the 16th Infantry Regiment, 22nd Infantry Division. Von Choltitz was an aggressive, 'up-front' style of infantry leader who played a key role in the capture of Fort Stalin and the assault crossing of Severnaya Bay. He was badly wounded in the right arm in the final days of the campaign. However, von Choltitz is best known for his role in the surrender of Paris in 1944. (Bundesarchiv, R63712)

BELOW
Oberst Otto Hitzfeld, commander of the 213th Infantry Regiment, 73rd Infantry Division. He was responsible for the capture of Fort Maxim Gorky I and was typical of the aggressive, very competent new type of German combat leaders that were emerging after a year on the Russian Front. (Bundesarchiv, 95/82/19)

command, Fretter-Pico was given XXX Corps. He was capable of conducting set-piece type attacks but lacked both the imagination and killer instinct that von Manstein desired from his subordinates and consequently, von Manstein kept turning to the more experienced Hansen to get the tough jobs done.

General der Kavallerie Erik Hansen (1889–1967). Hansen served as a junior cavalry officer on the Western Front in the opening phase of World War I, but then spent much of the war in staff positions. At the start of World War II, Hansen commanded the 4th Infantry Division in southern Poland and then was part of the exploitation force that followed the Panzers through the Sedan bridgehead into France in 1940. After the fall of France, Hansen served as chief of the Wehrmacht mission in Romania and then took command of LIV Corps in June 1941. It was his corps that conducted costly frontal assaults at Perekop and Ishun in 1941, and then maintained the siege of Sevastopol during the winter of 1941–42.

Von Manstein's seven divisional commanders during the siege of Sevastopol were an experienced group, most having combat command experience since 1939. **Generalmajor Ludwig Wolff** (1893–1968) was commander of the 22nd Infantry Division since October 1941. Wolff received the Knight's Cross in May 1941 as commander of the 192nd Infantry Regiment against the British Expeditionary Force in Belgium. **Generalleutnant Hans von Tettau** (1888–1956) was commander of the 24th Infantry Division since June 1940. Von Tettau had commanded a regiment at the start of the war and was given a division after the fall of France. **Generalleutnant Friedrich Schmidt** (1892–1943) was commander of the 50th Infantry Division since March 1942. Schmidt fought in World War I as a junior infantry officer but was not retained in the post-war Reichsheer. He rejoined the army in 1935 and commanded the 72nd Infantry Regiment (46th Infantry Division) in the 1939 Polish campaign. **Generalleutnant Fritz Lindemann** (1894–1944) was commander of the 132nd Infantry Division since 11 February 1942. Lindemann had seen a great deal of combat in 1939–41 as an artillery regiment commander in Poland, France and the drive on Moscow. The Gestapo later executed him for his participation in the 20 July plot

General-Major Ivan Efimovich Petrov (at far right), commander of the Coastal Army and Polkovnik Nikolai Gus, commander of the 345th Rifle Division. Petrov spent much of the campaign in his underground headquarters, and his ability to command was hindered by poor communications with front-line units under constant air and artillery attacks. (Author's collection)

against Hitler. **Generalleutnant Philipp Müller-Gebhard** (1889–1970) was commander of the 72nd Infantry Division since June 1941. Müller-Gebhard had fought in World War I as a junior infantry officer but was not selected to serve in the post-war Reichsheer. He returned to the army in 1934 and commanded a regiment in Poland. **Generalleutnant Johann Sinnhuber** (1887–1974) was commander of the 28th Light Division since May 1940. Sinnhuber was also an artilleryman with combat experience in World War I and Poland.

ROMANIAN

General-maior Gheorghe Avramescu (1884–1945) was commander of the Romanian Mountain Corps. Avramescu came from a peasant background but he succeeded in rising rapidly through the ranks of the Romanian Army, beginning as an infantry company commander during World War I. His corps had worked closely with the German Eleventh Army since the start of *Barbarossa* and Avramescu was quite familiar with German operational methods. However, Avramescu was resentful of von Manstein's tendency sometimes to order his Romanian units around directly or to detach them to the other German corps, thereby stripping Avramescu's headquarters down to a 'paper command' with no real subordinate units left. Avramescu was later executed by the Soviets in 1945.

SOVIET

The Soviet military leadership in Sevastopol did not reside in a single individual, but in the Black Sea Fleet's Military Council, which included Petrov and Oktyabrsky, as well as Coastal Artillery commander General-Major Petr A. Morgunov and Commissar N. M. Kulakov. Soviet commissars played a dominant role in the Crimea, since it was a semi-independent command and Stalin wanted to ensure that this key fortress city would not surrender. Decision making in the Sevastopol Defensive Region (SOR) was

General-Major Petr G. Novikov, commander of the 109th Rifle Division and Defensive Sector I near Balaklava. Novikov was the most experienced Soviet infantry commander at Sevastopol, having fought in Spain in 1937–38 and then Odessa in 1941. He was left 'holding the bag' at Sevastopol after Petrov and Oktyabrsky had fled and was captured, later being executed by the SS in 1944. (Author's collection)

based on communist committee-type methods, which allowed its participants to minimize personal blame for mistakes but was sluggish compared with German methods. Petrov and Oktyabrsky spent most of the siege in their underground headquarters in Sevastopol on South Bay.

General-Major Ivan Efimovich Petrov (1896–1958), commander of the Coastal Army since 19 August 1941. Petrov served mostly in Central Asia before the war and commanded the partly formed 27th Mechanized Corps at the start of the war. Once that command was disbanded, Petrov was sent to Odessa where he briefly commanded the pre-war 25th Rifle Division before taking over the Coastal Army. After Odessa was evacuated, Petrov's forces were en route to reinforce the 51st Army when the Germans broke through at Ishun. Petrov skilfully retreated his units to Sevastopol via Yalta, thereby avoiding being rounded up in the German pursuit. Although Oktyabrsky was commander of the SOR, Petrov was responsible for the bulk of the forces defending the city and he was the dominant command figure during the final German assault in 1942.

Vice-Admiral Filip S. Oktyabrsky (1899-1969), commander of the Black Sea Fleet since March 1939. Oktyabrsky had been in the Red Navy since 1918 and an early Communist Party member. From July to October 1941, Oktyabrsky conducted a brilliant defence of Odessa, inflicting heavy losses upon the Romanian Fourth Army, then saved most of his troops from capture in a well-handled evacuation of the city just as it was about to fall. He landed his troops in Sevastopol and took over the defence of that city just as von Manstein's troops were approaching the outskirts. Oktyabrsky was a tough defensive opponent and made good use of his naval gunfire and air support assets to bolster the defence.

General-Major Petr G. Novikov (1906–1944) was commander of the 109th Rifle Division and Defensive Sector I near Balaklava since 23 November 1941. Novikov was a tough, experienced infantry officer who had joined the Communist Party in 1928 and served as an adviser in Spain in 1937–38. At the outset of the war he commanded the 241st Rifle Regiment in the 95th Rifle Division and fought with that unit at Odessa. When Vice-Admiral Oktyabrsky was evacuated, Novikov briefly took over command of the SOR. Once the defence collapsed, Novikov attempted to escape on a cutter, but an enemy vessel intercepted his ship and he was captured. The SS later executed Novikov at Flossenberg concentration camp in 1944.

General-Major Trofim K. Kolomiets (1894–1971) was commander of the 25th Rifle Division since 1941. At Sevastopol, Kolomiets was also put in command of Defensive Sector III. Previously, he had two years commanding the 32nd Rifle Corps until it was destroyed in the Smolensk Pocket in July 1941. After escaping the fall of Sevastopol, Kolomiets took over command of the rebuilt 51st Army in July–October 1942.

Polkovnik Aleksandr G. Kapitokhin (1892–1958) was commander of the 95th Rifle Division and the critical Defensive Sector IV. After surviving the annihilation of his division at Sevastopol, Kapitokhin was given command of the 8th Guards Airborne Division in 1942–43. In 1943–44 he was made commander of all Soviet airborne troops.

Polkovnik Aleksandr G. Kapitokhin, commander of the 95th Rifle Division and Defensive Sector IV. Kapitokhin survived the destruction of his division at Sevastopol and went on to command Soviet airborne forces in 1943–44. (Author's collection)

Polkovnik N. F. Skutel'nik, commander of the 386th Rifle Division and Defensive Sector II. He faced the main weight of the German XXX Corps attack and he was wounded by German artillery in the decisive fight for the Sapun Ridge. (Author's collection)

OPPOSING FORCES

GERMAN

The German operational preference was to fight a war of manoeuvre but this was not possible at Sevastopol. Previous attacks on heavily fortified positions, such as Verdun in World War I or Brest-Litovsk in 1941 had proved both costly and time consuming, but von Manstein lacked both the time and the infantry reserves to fight a battle of attrition. Instead, he hoped to use a combination of firepower and combat multipliers, as well as the judicious use of infantry assaults, to gradually undermine and crack open the Soviet defensive belts at Sevastopol.

Infantry and assault guns

The German XXX and LIV Corps could muster seven infantry divisions with a total of 57 infantry battalions for *Störfang*. While the German infantrymen were experienced and confident of victory, the heavy losses of the first year of the war had worn down most units considerably. Von Manstein did succeed in getting OKH to provide his army with a significant number of infantry replacements just prior to the attack on Sevastopol, but the Eleventh Army's infantry units were starting the attack at anywhere from 35 to 75 per cent strength in personnel.[1] Most of the infantry battalions had a fighting strength of only 300–400 troops in early June 1942, and the 170th Infantry Division had to cannibalize one of its infantry regiments to bring the other two up to combat strength. Thus, the German infantry was a fragile force at Sevastopol and von Manstein could not afford to squander it if he wanted to keep the offensive going. Furthermore, German infantry tactical doctrine stressed bypassing strongpoints but since this was not possible at Sevastopol, the Germans were forced to reduce one strongpoint after another. To support the infantry, von Manstein provided three battalions of assault guns with about 65 StuG IIIs armed with short-barrelled 75mm guns, useful against bunkers. Infantry assault groups typically were based around a battalion, with a platoon of engineers, a few assault guns and some *Panzerjäger* in direct support.

Assault pioneers

Assault pioneers would spearhead the offensive, breaching minefields, destroying obstacles and dealing with a maze of bunkers, trenches and caves.

1. In LIV Corps, the 22nd Infantry Division was the strongest since it was short only 1,750 personnel, while the 132nd Infantry Division was the weakest since it was short over 2,800 personnel.

The Germans used a hotchpotch of captured heavy artillery at Sevastopol, including this elderly single trail howitzer. Despite all the publicity given to prestige weapons such as 'Dora' and the Karl mortars, the Germans had great difficulty assembling a proper siege train at Sevastopol. (HITM Photo Research)

Von Manstein assigned two pioneer battalions to each of his attacking infantry divisions (the extra battalions were stripped from other units) as a combat multiplier. The eight pioneer battalions supporting LIV Corps had an average fighting strength of 386 men. Each pioneer battalion was equipped with 10–12 flame-throwers, 28–30 mine-detectors, 3,000kg of high explosives (including 6–8 50kg and 16 12.5kg hollow charges for use against fortifications), 2,200 hand grenades and 500 smoke grenades. The German pioneer units also tended to be in better shape than their infantry counterparts, with two to three officers and six to eight NCOs per company, versus only one officer and three NCOs in most infantry companies in LIV Corps. For clearing Soviet obstacles, the German pioneers would also be assisted by the 300th Panzer Battalion (FL), a remote-controlled tank unit employing the new B IV and Goliath explosive carriers for the first time.

Artillery

For the assault upon Sevastopol, the Eleventh Army assembled the largest collection of artillery pieces under a single command by the German Army in World War II. The 306th Army Artillery Command (Harko 306) under General der Artillerie Johannes Zuckertort directed the Eleventh Army artillery assets, as well as those of the LIV Corps and their subordinate divisions. The 110th Army Artillery Command (Harko 110) under General der Artillerie Robert Martinek directed the much smaller XXX Corps artillery. Together, the 110th and 306th Army Artillery Commands controlled about 785 German and 112 Romanian medium and heavy guns, of which most supported the main effort, that of LIV Corps.

Much of the attention about Axis artillery at Sevastopol has focused on two 'celebrity' weapons – the Karl 600mm heavy mortars and the 800mm railway gun 'Dora'. The 833rd Heavy Mortar Battery under Major Freiherr Rüdt von Collenberg with two 600mm Karl mortars – dubbed 'Thor' and 'Odin' arrived by rail near Sevastopol and were in their firing positions by 20 May.[2] Although the 2.4-ton concrete-piercing shells were capable of smashing any fortifications they could hit, the Karl had a number of weaknesses that made it less than ideal as a battlefield support weapon. The

---

2. The battery may have arrived with a spare Karl mortar, but only 'Odin' and 'Thor' were used.

In 1935, Oberst Erich von Manstein submitted a proposal for mobile assault artillery units to provide direct-fire support for German infantry divisions. This proposal eventually resulted in the deployment of the Sturmgeschütz III Ausf. A assault gun in 1940, armed with a short-barrelled 75mm StuK 37 L/24 gun. Von Manstein would get to apply his pre-war concept in action at Sevastopol, where Eleventh Army had three assault gun battalions at its disposal. (Nik Cornish Archive, WH579)

entire Karl tracked weapon system weighed 124 tons, which made it rather clumsy and, even worse, the weapon had a range of only 4,000m which made it vulnerable to Soviet counterbattery fire. The single 800mm railway gun 'Dora' belonging to the 672nd Artillery Battalion was even more impractical since it required days of engineer work to both assemble the weapon and construct a firing position. 'Dora', the largest artillery piece ever built, could fire a 7.1-ton concrete-piercing shell out to 37km or a 4.8-ton high explosive shell out to 47km. While the size of both the Karl mortars and 'Dora' were superficially impressive, neither weapon was particularly accurate and their rate of fire was very slow. Furthermore, only 122 rounds of 600mm and 48 rounds of 800mm were stockpiled at the start of *Störfang* and both systems had expended most of their ammunition before the infantry assault had made much progress.

Somewhat more useful for the 306th Amy Artillery Command were the two 'Long Bruno' 283mm railroad guns of the 688th Railway Artillery Battery, the two 420mm howitzers of the 458th and 459th Heavy Artillery Batteries, and the two 355mm howitzers and four 305mm mortars of the 641st Artillery Battalion. Both of the 420mm howitzers were World War I-era weapons that were powerful but short ranged and only provided with enough ammunition for the initial attacks. The nine 283mm howitzers in the 741st, 742nd, 743rd and 744th Artillery Battalions were all pre- World War I weapons and six of the weapons had burst barrels after two weeks' firing. In contrast, the 355mm M1 howitzers, 240mm H39 howitzers and 283mm 'Long Brunos' were capable of better range and accuracy. However, it is apparent that the Eleventh Army's heavy artillery was a rather hotchpotch collection of modern and obsolete, foreign-made and German-made weapons and this lack of standardization hindered both fire planning and resupply. Except for the Czech-made 305mm mortars and 240mm howitzers, none of the large-calibre weapons had an adequate ammunition supply for sustained operations.

Of course the bulk of fire support for *Störfang* was provided by the standard medium-calibre German corps and division-level artillery. The 306th Army Artillery Command controlled about 268 105mm l.FH 18 and 80 150mm s.FH 18 howitzers, as well as the 1st and 2nd Nebelwerfer Regiments with 126 multiple rocket launchers. While the medium artillery was generally less effective against concrete fortifications, it was fairly effective against trenches and earth bunkers. At the start of *Störfang* the 306th Army Artillery Command had stockpiled 183,750 rounds of 105mm and 47,300 rounds of 150mm ammunition, enough for 12 days' firing.

ROMANIAN

The Romanian Mountain Corps attached to the Eleventh Army comprised the 1st and 4th Mountain Divisions and the 18th Infantry Division. Altogether, the Romanian Army contributed 18 infantry battalions and one machine-gun battalion to the assault on Sevastopol – about a quarter of the Axis total. Romanian infantry were fairly well armed, including eight ZB54 7.92mm machine guns and four 81mm mortars in each battalion. The Romanian mountain infantry (*vanatori de munte*) were regarded as elite troops, particularly the 1st Mountain Division, which had performed well in the initial assault upon Sevastopol in December 1941. However, the 18th Infantry Division was composed of reservists and had seen little action before *Störfang*. While the Romanians had plentiful infantry, X Mountain Corps was weak in artillery and combat engineers. The Mountain Corps had an initial total of 112 guns in 12 artillery battalions (55 75/76mm, 20 100mm, two 122mm, 33 150mm, two 152mm), but more than half were obsolescent French- and Czech-made 75mm guns, which lacked the 'punch' to neutralize Soviet fortifications. The only decent fire support available was the corps-level motorized heavy artillery regiment. The weakness of the Romanian artillery had inhibited their siege of Odessa in 1941 and reduced the independent offensive potential of the Mountain Corps at Sevastopol. The Germans were making efforts to re-equip the Romanian 18th Infantry Division with captured Soviet artillery, but at the start of *Störfang* only one battalion had been re-equipped. Furthermore, the Romanian corps only had the equivalent of two weak pioneer battalions. The Romanians were brave, aggressive soldiers capable of conducting set-piece attacks, but the lack of combat support assets made them highly dependent upon the Germans to conduct effective offensive operations.

A Romanian machine-gun team with a 7.92mm ZB 53 Model 1937 heavy machine gun. A total of eight of these guns were assigned to the heavy weapons company in each Romanian infantry battalion. (Nik Cornish Archive, WH662)

SOVIET

The siege of Sevastopol forced the Soviets to fight a joint army–navy campaign from the start, with the Black Sea Fleet and the Independent Coastal Army sharing the responsibility for the defence of the city.

Naval infantry
During 1941–42, the Black Sea Fleet sent 49,372 personnel to fight as naval infantry (*Morskaya Pekhota*). Unlike true marines, the naval infantry were not previously trained for ground combat and were essentially ad hoc units formed as an emergency measure.

ABOVE
There were over 12,000 naval infantry in Sevastopol in the spring of 1942, comprising 14 per cent of the garrison. Note that this is a mixed unit, with both troops from a naval rifle brigade wearing steel helmets and sailors from an ad hoc battalion wearing soft caps. Also note the barrel of a 130mm naval gun in the background; a number of these weapons were taken from damaged warships and put in extemporized ground mounts. (Central Museum of the Armed Forces, Moscow)

ABOVE RIGHT
Soviet naval infantry with a 120mm mortar. The 79th Naval Infantry Brigade had a battery of eight 120mm mortars and they could engage targets out to 5,700m. Typically, these mortar batteries occupied reverse slope positions in ravines and were difficult for the Germans to pinpoint. (Central Museum of the Armed Forces, Moscow)

However, the naval infantry units did play a major role in the defence of Sevastopol, with the 7th, 8th and 79th Naval Infantry Brigades stopping the German offensive in December 1941. Once Operation *Störfang* began, the Soviets quickly transported the 9th Naval Infantry Brigade and the 138th and 142nd Naval Rifle Brigades into Sevastopol to bolster the defence.[3] The Naval infantry brigades were quite large, typically having four to six infantry battalions with up to 4,000 infantrymen, which gave these units the ability to absorb significant losses. Naval infantrymen were also armed with the modern SVT-40 semi-automatic rifle, which was significantly better than the elderly Mosin-Nagant bolt-action rifles carried by the Soviet Army. In June 1942, the 79th Naval Infantry Brigade had just completed refitting with 3,500 troops in its three rifle battalions, a mortar battalion (26 82mm and eight 120mm mortars), an anti-tank battery (six 45mm guns) and an artillery battalion (eight 76mm guns and four 122mm howitzers). The three rifle battalions in the brigade were armed with 94 light and 38 heavy machine guns and 35 50mm mortars – a considerable amount of firepower. At Sevastopol, about 20 per cent of the troops in the Coastal Army were naval infantry and they generally proved to be stubborn defensive fighters. However, the 138th and 142nd Naval Infantry Brigades, which included significant numbers of Muslim troops from the Caucasus, were plagued by desertions. Sailors also manned the armoured train 'Zhelezniakov', which mounted four 76mm naval guns – and which provided mobile firepower support throughout the siege.

Independent Coastal Army

At the start of June 1942, the Soviet Independent Coastal Army consisted of seven rifle divisions and four naval infantry brigades, which had the equivalent of perhaps 75 infantry battalions. The strongest units were the 95th, 109th, 172nd and 388th Rifle Divisions which each had about 7,000 troops, while the other divisions each had about 5,000 troops. Thanks to the efforts of the Black Sea Fleet, the Coastal Army received 5,000 replacements just two weeks prior to *Störfang*, as well as major shipments of fuel and ammunition. Petrov's infantry had the advantage of defending prepared positions and the troops were fairly experienced. However, Petrov's army was relatively weak in supporting arms – only two battalions of T-26 light tanks, limited numbers of

3. Naval rifle brigades (*Morskaya Strelkovy*) were composed of naval personnel but organized by the Red Army on standard rifle unit organization.

engineers and anti-aircraft troops – which made efforts to counterattack difficult. Petrov's artillery park was considerable, with 455 guns and howitzers (including at least 34 152mm and 40 122mm howitzers) and 918 mortars. Initially, the ammunition supply was adequate for a battle of up to two weeks, with three to four basic loads available for most heavy weapons but 82mm mortar ammunition was in short supply. Poor communications between headquarters in Sevastopol and the forward positions further hampered Petrov's ability to respond to German attacks against his perimeter in a timely manner. Instead, the infantry battalions relied upon their organic 82mm and 50mm mortars to repel German attacks.

A typical unit such as the 109th Rifle Division had about 7,500 troops at the start of the German offensive, of which almost 80 per cent were assigned to its infantry and artillery battalions. In the 109th Rifle Division, 43 per cent of the troops were Russian, 27 per cent were Ukrainian, 8 per cent Georgian, 5 per cent Azerbaijanis and 17 per cent other minorities. Each Soviet rifle battalion generally had three rifle companies (each with 50–120 troops, three to seven light machine guns, up to two heavy machine guns and three to four 50mm mortars), a heavy machine-gun company and a mortar battery. Food shortages were an issue and would severely sap the strength of Soviet combat units.

By the time that Störfang began, the Soviets had built hundreds of simple but effective earth and timber bunkers, which typically held a four-man machine-gun crew or a single 45mm anti-tank gun. These bunkers were difficult to spot and usually required point-blank fire to destroy them. Reinforced concrete bunkers were less frequent, with only 19 scattered along the 37km of the outer defensive belt. Soviet engineers also laid thousands of PMD-6 wooden anti-personnel mines and TMD 40 wooden anti-tank mines, as well as dense barbed-wire obstacle belts.

Coastal defence forces

General-Major Petr Morgunov's Coastal Artillery force was a semi-independent command for much of the siege but was integrated into the defence. In October 1941, the Coastal Artillery had 12 batteries with 45 guns, but more were added during the siege. The Coastal Defence force was capable of placing very heavy fire upon German targets but limited barrel life and small stocks of remaining ammunition reduced their role by the time of the final assault upon Sevastopol. At the start of Störfang, Morgunov had 51 guns available (eight 305mm, one 180mm, 10 152mm, 17 130mm, three 120mm, eight 100mm and four 45mm).

The Soviet flotilla leader *Tashkent*, which made repeated supply runs into Sevastopol in 1941–42. This ship was built in Italy and delivered in February 1939 with three single 130mm guns but was upgraded with three twin turrets by the start of the war, Known as the 'Blue Cruiser' because of her unusual sky blue paint. (Author's collection)

ORDERS OF BATTLE, 2 JUNE 1942

AXIS

ELEVENTH ARMY, 2 JUNE 1942
(GENERALFELDMARSCHALL ERICH VON MANSTEIN)

Army troops:

672nd Artillery Battalion ('Dora')

833rd Heavy Artillery Battalion (Karl)

672nd Artillery Battalion (420mm)

688th Railway Artillery Battery

474th Artillery Battalion

707th Artillery Battalion

741st Artillery Battalion

742nd Artillery Battalion

743rd Artillery Battalion

744th Artillery Battalion

I/814th Artillery Battalion

II/814th Artillery Battalion

II/818th Artillery Battalion

458th Heavy Artillery Battery

459th Heavy Artillery Battery

XXX ARMY CORPS (GENERAL DER ARTILLERIE MAXIMILIAN FRETTER-PICO)

Corps troops:

110th Army Artillery Command (General der Artillerie Robert Martinek)

    I/70th Nebelwerfer Battalion

    II/70th Nebelwerfer Battalion

    II/Artillerie Lehr Regiment

    7th Romanian Heavy Artillery Regiment

3rd Company, 300th Panzer Battalion (Remote Control) [4]

70th Pioneer Battalion

741st Pioneer Battalion

902nd Assault Boat Command

249th Assault Gun Battalion (14 x StuG III)

28th Light Division (General der Infanterie Johann Sinnhuber)

    49th Jäger Regiment

    83rd Jäger Regiment

    28th Artillery Regiment

    28th Pioneer Battalion

72nd Infantry Division (General der Artillerie Philipp Müller-Gebhard)

    105th Infantry Regiment

    124th Infantry Regiment

    266th Infantry Regiment

    172nd Artillery Regiment

    172nd Pioneer Battalion

170th Infantry Division (Generalleutnant Erwin Sander)

    391st Infantry Regiment

    399th Infantry Regiment [5]

    240th Artillery Regiment

    240th Pioneer Battalion

    240th Bicycle Battalion [6]

LIV ARMY CORPS
(GENERAL DER KAVALLERIE ERIK HANSEN)

Corps troops:

306th Army Artillery Command (General der Artillerie Johannes Zuckertort)

    1st Heavy Nebelwerfer Regiment

    II/Nebelwerfer Lehr Regiment 1

    1st Nebelwerfer Battalion

    4th Nebelwerfer Battalion

1st and 2nd Companies, 300th Panzer Battalion (RC)

46th Pioneer Battalion

71st Pioneer Battalion

88th Pioneer Battalion

173rd Pioneer Battalion

744th Pioneer Battalion

905th Assault Boat Command

190th Assault Gun Battalion

197th Assault Gun Battalion

22nd Infantry Division (Generalmajor Ludwig Wolff)

    16th Infantry Regiment

    47th Infantry Regiment

    65th Infantry Regiment

    22nd Artillery Regiment

    22nd Pioneer Battalion

24th Infantry Division (Generalleutnant Hans von Tettau)

    31st Infantry Regiment

    32nd Infantry Regiment

    102nd Infantry Regiment

    24th Artillery Regiment

    24th Pioneer Battalion

50th Infantry Division (Generalleutnant Friedrich Schmidt)

    121st Infantry Regiment

    122nd Infantry Regiment

    123rd Infantry Regiment

    150th Artillery Battalion

    IV/173rd Artillery Battalion

    624th Artillery Battalion

    737th Artillery Battalion

    150th Pioneer Battalion

132nd Infantry Division (Generalleutnant Fritz Lindemann)

    436th Infantry Regiment

437th Infantry Regiment – only two battalions present
438th Infantry Regiment – only two battalions present
132nd Artillery Regiment
III/111th Artillery Battalion
I/173rd Artillery Battalion
IV/150th Artillery Battalion
815th Artillery Battalion
132nd Pioneer Battalion
213th Infantry Regiment from 73rd Infantry Division –
only two battalions present

ROMANIAN MOUNTAIN CORPS
(GENERAL-MAIOR GHEORGHE AVRAMESCU)

57th Heavy Artillery Battalion
53rd Mountain Artillery Regiment

1st Mountain Division (General de brigadă Constantin Rascanu)
    1st Mountain Rifle Regiment
    2nd Mountain Rifle Regiment
    1st Mountain Artillery Regiment

18th Infantry Division (General-maior Radu Băldescu)
    18th Infantry Regiment
    90th Infantry Regiment
    92nd Infantry Regiment
    35th Field Artillery Regiment
    36th Field Artillery Regiment
    18th Engineer Battalion
    33rd Infantry Regiment/10th Infantry Division [7]

LUFTWAFFE
Flieger Korps VIII (Generaloberst von Richthofen):
Fighters (100):
    III/Jagdgeschwader 3 Udet (27x Bf 109F)
    II/Jagdgeschwader 77 (36 x Bf 109F)
    III/Jagdgeschwader 77 (37 x Bf 109F)
Bombers (168):
    I/Kampfgeschwader 51 Edelweiss (35 x Ju 88)
    I/Kampfgeschwader 76 (31 x Ju 88)
    III/Kampfgeschwader 76 (29 x Ju 88A, 12 x Ju 88C)
    I/Kampfgeschwader 100 Wiking (34 x He 111H)
    III/Lehrgeschwader 1 (27 x Ju 88)
Ground attack (73):
    Stab/Sturzkampfgeschwader 77 (three x Ju 87, 6 x Bf 110)
    I/Sturzkampfgeschwader 77 (37 x Ju 87B or D)
    II/Sturzkampfgeschwader 77 (27 x Ju 87)
Reconnaissance (24):
    3.(Heer)/11 (10 x Bf 110C/D/E)
    3.(Heer)/13 (14 x HS 126B)
    Fliegerführer Süd (Oberst von Wild)
    II/Kampfgeschwader 26 (45 x He 111H-6 torpedo bombers)

KRIEGSMARINE
1st S-Boat Flotilla (*S-26, S-27, S-28, S-40, S-72, S-102*)
(Kapitänleutnant Heinz Birnbacher)

ITALIAN REGIA MARINA
101st MAS Boat Flotilla (*MAS570, MAS571, MAS572, MAS573*)
Submarines (*CB3, CB5*)

SOVIET
INDEPENDENT COASTAL ARMY
(GENERAL-MAJOR IVAN E. PETROV)
Commander, Sevastopol Defence Region –
Vice-Admiral Filip S. Oktyabrsky
Commander, Black Sea Coastal Defences –
General-Major Petr A. Morgunov

Army troops:
9th Naval Infantry Brigade, Polkovnik N. V. Blagovestchenskiy
2nd Battalion, 745th Rifle Regiment
'Sevastopol' Garrison Regiment
81st Separate Tank Battalion (1 x T-34, 12 x T-26 and BT-7)
125th Separate Tank Battalion, Major Listobayev (25 x T-26S)
18th Guards Artillery Regiment
52nd Artillery Regiment
101st Artillery Regiment
134th Artillery Regiment
700th Artillery Regiment
69th Howitzer Regiment
265th Artillery Regiment (mot.)
Armoured Train 'Zhelezniakov'
2nd Anti-Aircraft Regiment
61st Anti-Aircraft Regiment
323rd Anti-Aircraft Regiment
880th Anti-Aircraft Regiment
26th Anti-Aircraft Battalion
138th Anti-Tank Battalion
174th Anti-Tank Battalion
176th Anti-Tank Battalion

Defensive Sector I:
109th Rifle Division (General-Major Petr G. Novikov)
    381st Rifle Regiment
    456th NKVD Regiment
    602nd Rifle Regiment
    404th Artillery Regiment
    109th Anti-Tank Battalion

388th Rifle Division (Polkovnik Monakhov)
    773rd Rifle Regiment
    778th Rifle Regiment
    782nd Rifle Regiment
    953rd Artillery Regiment

675th Mortar Battalion
677th Anti-Aircraft Battalion
671st Pioneer Battalion

Defensive Sector II:
386th Rifle Division (Polkovnik N. F. Skutel'nik)
    769th Rifle Regiment
    772nd Rifle Regiment
    775th Rifle Regiment
    952nd Artillery Regiment
    U/I mortar battalion
    675th Anti-Aircraft Battalion
    670th Pioneer Battalion)

7th Naval Infantry Brigade (Polkovnik Y. I. Zhidilov)
    1st Rifle Battalion
    2nd Rifle Battalion
    3rd Rifle Battalion
    5th Rifle Battalion
    6th Rifle Battalion

Defensive Sector III:
25th 'Chapaevskaya' Rifle Division (General-Major
Trofim K. Kolomiets)
    31st Rifle Regiment
    54th Rifle Regiment
    287th Rifle Regiment
    3rd Naval Infantry Regiment
    2nd Perekop Regiment
    99th Artillery Regiment
    756th Mortar Battalion
    164th Anti-Tank Battalion
    105th Pioneer Battalion

345th Rifle Division (Polkovnik Nikolai Gus)
    1163rd Rifle Regiment
    1165th Rifle Regiment
    1167th Rifle Regiment
    905th Artillery Regiment
    674th Anti-Tank Battalion
    629th Anti-Aircraft Battalion
    622nd Pioneer Battalion

8th Naval Infantry Brigade (Polkovnik P. F. Gorpishchenko)

79th Naval Infantry Brigade (Polkovnik A. S. Potapov)
    1st Rifle Battalion
    2nd Rifle Battalion
    3rd Rifle Battalion
    Mortar Battalion
    Artillery Battalion

Defensive Sector IV:
95th Rifle Division (Polkovnik Aleksandr G. Kapitokhin)
    90th Rifle Regiment
    161st Rifle Regiment
    241st Rifle Regiment
    57th Artillery Regiment
    757th Mortar Battalion
    97th Anti-Tank Battalion
    48th Pioneer Battalion

172nd Rifle Division (Polkovnik Ivan Laskin)
    383rd Rifle Regiment
    514th Rifle Regiment
    747th Rifle Regiment
    134th Howitzer Regiment
    247th Pioneer Battalion
    School Battalion[8]
    758th Mortar Battalion
    674th Anti-Tank Regiment[9]
    141st School Regiment (two battalions)

SOVIET AIR FORCE – BLACK SEA FLEET (VOYENNO-VOZDUSHNYE SILY – CHERNOMORSKIY FLOT, VVS-CHF)
3rd OAG (Special Aviation Group) (Polkovnik G. G. Dzyuba)
6th Guards Naval Fighter Regiment (Yak-1)
(Polkovnik K. I. Yumashev)
9th Naval Fighter Regiment
247th Fighter Regiment (LaGG-3, I-16, I-153)
18th Ground Attack Regiment (10 Il-2) (Polkovnik A. A. Gubriy)
23rd Aviation Regiment (U-2 and UT-1 biplane light bombers)
116th Maritime Reconnaissance Regiment (MBR-2 flying boats)
32nd Guards Fighter Regiment

SOVIET BLACK SEA FLEET UNITS INVOLVED IN SUPPORTING SEVASTOPOL
Heavy Cruisers (2): *Molotov, Voroshilov*
Light Cruisers (1): *Krasny Krym*
Flotilla Leaders (2): *Tashkent, Kharkov*
Destroyers (6): *Svobodny, Soobrazitelny, Bditelny, Bezuprechny, Nezamozhnik, Dzerzhinskiy*
Minesweepers (9): *T401, T403, T404, T407–T411, T413*
Guardships (1): *Shkval*
Submarines (24): *L-23, L-24, S-31, S-32, M31, M32, M33, M60, M112, M117, M118, Shch 209, Shch 212, Shch 213, Shch 214, Shch 205, Shch 208, M52, L-4, L-5, D-4, D-5, A-2, A-4*

4. This unit had two companies of PzKpfw III Ausf. J tanks, as well as the following remote-control vehicles: four x NSU Kettenrad, *c.*25 x B IV heavy explosive carriers (SdKfz 301), *c.*15x Goliath (SdKfz 302), unknown number of R/C Bren gun carriers and Vickers Utility tractors.
5. The 401st Infantry Regiment was nominally part of the division but had been stripped of personnel to reinforce the other two regiments and was a mere cadre during *Störfang*.
6. Reconnaissance battalion with armoured cars.
7. Attached to the German 24th Infantry Division, 7–12 June 1942.
8. One rifle company, one machine-gun company, one mortar company.
9. Five batteries of 76.2mm anti-tank guns.

OPERATION *TRAPPENJAGD,* 8–21 MAY 1942

Before dealing with Sevastopol, von Manstein decided to deal with the three Soviet armies located in the Kerch Peninsula, which had been constantly trying to break out. Leaving only Hansen's LIV Corps to watch Sevastopol, von Manstein massed five German infantry divisions, one Panzer division and two-and-a-half Romanian divisions to attack a total of 19 Soviet divisions and four armoured brigades in the Kerch Peninsula.

The Soviet Crimean Front under General-Lieutenant Dmitri T. Kozlov appeared formidable, with three lines of defence. It deployed General-Lieutenant Vladimir N. L'vov's 51st Army (eight rifle divisions, three rifle brigades and two tank brigades) in the northern sector of the peninsula and the 44th Army under General-Lieutenant Stepan I. Cherniak (five rifle divisions and two tank brigades) to guard the southern sector of the front along the Black Sea. The 47th Army under General-Major Konstantin S. Kolganov had four rifle divisions and one cavalry division as front reserves. Kozlov did not expect a major German attack given that his forces outnumbered the enemy by more than two to one and the swampy terrain along the Black Sea coast appeared unfavourable for offensive operations.

Von Manstein's offensive, named *Trappenjagd* (Bustard Hunt), used General Fretter-Pico's XXX Corps, to attack the 44th Army on the southern coast. Von Manstein intended to smash in the weaker left wing and then pivot north with 22nd Panzer Division to trap the main Soviet forces against the Sea of Azov. Operation *Trappenjagd* began at 0415hrs on 8 May 1942, with a ten-minute artillery barrage against the Soviet 44th Army. In only three-and-a-half hours, the 44th Army's front-line units were shattered and their second line of defence pierced. The collapse of the 44th Army was accelerated by a seaborne assault using the assault boats from the 902nd Assault Boat Command to land a reinforced infantry company from the 436th Infantry Regiment (132nd Infantry Division) 1.5km behind the main Soviet obstacle belt. This was an extremely bold move and it helped to unhinge the Soviet second line of defence. Once the main obstacle belt was breached, von Manstein ordered the mobile Groddeck Brigade to move

A German railway gun fires at Sevastopol, March 1942. Hansen's LIV Corps had to keep the pressure on Petrov's garrison during the spring, while von Manstein dealt with the larger threat in the Kerch Peninsula. (HITM Photo Research)

through the breach and link up with the 436th Infantry Regiment's beachhead and then advance eastward. In short order, the 44th Army's flank collapsed. Although XXX Corps had suffered 104 killed and 284 wounded on the first day of *Trappenjagd* it had captured 4,514 prisoners.

Meanwhile, Fliegerkorps VIII launched a series of devastating attacks upon the VVS forward airfields in the Crimea and the Taman Peninsula, destroying over 100 Soviet aircraft.

The day of decision for Operation *Trappenjagd* was 9 May and it quickly went badly for Kozlov's Crimean Front. Kozlov did not fully appreciate the German breakthrough in the 44th Army sector and failed to commit sufficient reserves to counterattack the penetration. On the afternoon of 9 May, the Groddeck Brigade overran the Marfovka airfield, destroying 35 I-153 fighters on the ground. Kozlov was flabbergasted and the fear that Germans were running amok in the rear areas helped to shatter Soviet morale.

At that point, von Manstein committed the 22nd Panzer Division, which attacked northward and quickly pinned the bulk of the 51st Army against the Sea of Azov. Once this happened, Soviet command and control completely collapsed and a disorganized stampede to the rear began.

The eight divisions of the encircled 51st Army soon surrendered, which released XXX Corps to pursue the retreating Soviet fragments. Kozlov attempted to organize an evacuation from Kerch, but by 14 May the 170th Infantry Division had fought its way into the west side of the city. The final Soviet pockets near Kerch were finally annihilated on 20 May by massed German artillery and bomber attacks. In the end, the Soviets only evacuated 37,000 troops from Kerch before it fell.

In one of the more astonishing victories of World War II, von Manstein had smashed three Soviet armies in less than two weeks. The Crimean Front suffered about 28,000 dead and 147,000 captured, with nine out of 18 divisions completely destroyed. All the Soviet tanks and artillery in the Kerch Peninsula had been lost as well as 417 aircraft. German losses were relatively light, a total of 3,397 casualties in XXX and XLII Corps (including 600 dead), as well as eight tanks, three assault guns and nine artillery pieces. More significant was the expenditure of 6,230 tons of ammunition, which would require almost two weeks for Eleventh Army to replenish. Although von Manstein had to return the 22nd Panzer Division and some of the Luftwaffe units to Army Group South for the counterattacks at Kharkov, he could now turn to deal exclusively with fortress Sevastopol for the first time.

BELOW RIGHT
German infantry from the 50th Infantry Division march through a small Crimean village en route to Sevastopol in late May 1942 after their successful role in Operation *Trappenjagd* in the Kerch Peninsula. (HITM Photo Research)

BELOW
Soviet prisoners in the Kerch area after the conclusion of Operation *Trappenjagd*. The Eleventh Army captured about 147,000 prisoners in less than two weeks. The annihilation of the Soviet armies in the Kerch Peninsula meant that the Sevastopol garrison was on its own. (Anne S. K. Brown)

Operation *Trappenjagd*, 8 May 1942

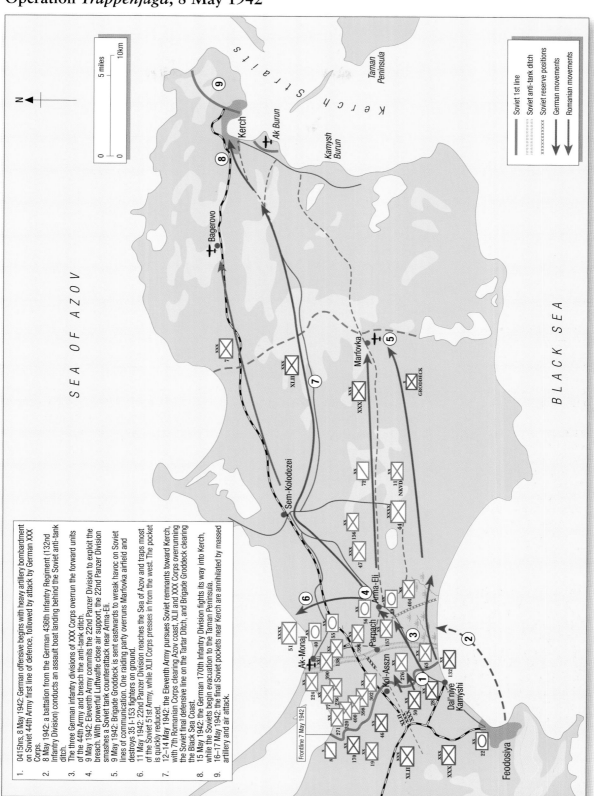

1. 0415hrs, 8 May 1942: German offensive begins with heavy artillery bombardment on Soviet 44th Army first line of defence, followed by attack by German XXX Corps.
2. 8 May 1942: a battalion from the German 436th Infantry Regiment (132nd Infantry Division) conducts an assault boat landing behind the Soviet anti-tank ditch.
3. The three German infantry divisions of XXX Corps overrun the forward units of the 44th Army and breach the anti-tank ditch.
4. 9 May 1942: Eleventh Army commits the 22nd Panzer Division to exploit the breach. With powerful Luftwaffe close air support, the 22nd Panzer Division smashes a Soviet tank counterattack near Arma-Eli.
5. 9 May 1942: Brigade Groddeck is sent eastwards to wreak havoc on Soviet lines of communication. One raiding party overruns Marfovka airfield and destroys 35 I-153 fighters on ground.
6. 11 May 1942: 22nd Panzer Division reaches the Sea of Azov and traps most of the Soviet 51st Army, while XLII Corps presses in from the west. The pocket is quickly reduced.
7. 12–14 May 1942: the Eleventh Army pursues Soviet remnants toward Kerch, with 7th Romanian Corps clearing Azov coast, XLII and XXX Corps overrunning the Soviet final defensive line on the Tartar Ditch, and Brigade Groddeck clearing the Black Sea Coast.
8. 15 May 1942: the German 170th Infantry Division fights its way into Kerch, while the Soviets begin evacuation to the Taman Peninsula.
9. 16–17 May 1942: the final Soviet pockets near Kerch are annihilated by massed artillery and air attack.

AIR AND NAVAL OPERATIONS AROUND SEVASTOPOL 1941–42

AIR OPERATIONS

In late October 1941, the air and air defence assets available to defend Sevastopol were modest. The air defence of Sevastopol was the responsibility of the Black Sea Fleet's air arm – the VVS-CHF, which formed the 3rd OAG (Special Aviation Group). The 3rd OAG's main component was the 62nd Fighter Brigade, which on 7 November 1941 had 32 modern fighters (Yak-1, MiG-3, LaGG-3) and 39 obsolescent fighters (I-16, I-153), based at the small dirt strip near the Chersonese Lighthouse. Close air support was provided by small detachments with six Il-2 'Sturmoviks'. Initially, three anti-aircraft battalions formed the basis for Sevastopol's air defence, with 160 medium-calibre guns (76mm and 85mm), 36 small-calibre guns (37mm and 45mm) and one anti-aircraft machine-gun unit with 18 Maxim M-4 quadruple machine guns.

In November 1941, the Luftwaffe was only able to move one *Jagdgruppe* from Jagdgeschwader (JG) 77 and one Stuka group from Sturzkampfgeschwader (StG) 77 to Sarabus airstrip, near Evpatoria. The rest of the Luftwaffe bombers from Fliegerkorps IV had to operate from fields in the Ukraine. The

A Ju 87B Stuka dive-bombing a target. Von Richthofen's Fliegerkorps VIII started the attack on Sevastopol with 67 Ju 87 Stuka's from StG 77, of which typically 75 per cent were operational. (HITM Photo Research)

3rd OAG immediately began to launch a series of raids on Sarabus Airstrip in order to prevent the Luftwaffe from making the base fully operational. Most of the Soviet attacks involved only 8–12 aircraft, but they succeeded in inflicting some painful losses. Meanwhile, the Luftwaffe was able to bring in enough aircraft to mount regular attacks on Sevastopol's naval dockyards, causing damage to both shipping and shore facilities.

In addition to interdiction strikes against Sarabus and German lines of communication through Simferopol, the Soviet naval aviators mounted combat air patrols over the city and provided occasional close air support to units on the front line. Soviet naval fighters in Sevastopol flew over 1,000 sorties in November 1941, losing 33 aircraft and claiming 54 German aircraft. Fliegerkorps IV's limited assets were split between providing close air support to the Eleventh Army, naval interdiction missions, laying magnetic mines off Sevastopol and supply operations. However, the small force of Bf 109F fighters from III/JG 77 could not gain air superiority over Sevastopol in November 1941.

Fliegerkorps IV returned to the Crimea in mid-December to support von Manstein's second attack upon Sevastopol and committed 60 bombers, 25 Stukas and 25 Bf 109s to the offensive. During air operations in December 1941, the Luftwaffe destroyed 17 Soviet aircraft around Sevastopol, but lost 13 of its own. After the failure of von Manstein's December offensive, Fliegerkorps IV left the Crimea and the Soviets regained air superiority over Sevastopol.

In May 1942, Generaloberst von Richthofen's Fliegerkorps VIII moved to the Crimean theatre and rapidly gained air superiority over the Kerch Peninsula and paved the way for the success of Operation *Trappenjagd*. Once the Soviet lodgement in the Kerch Peninsula was eliminated, Fliegerkorps VIII turned its attentions to Sevastopol. Since the winter, the Soviets had augmented the air group with the 6th Guards Naval Fighter Regiment (Yak-1) and detachments from two other fighter units, but the three small airstrips inside the Sevastopol perimeter could only accommodate about 50 aircraft at once.

For the final assault of Sevastopol, Fliegerkorps VIII committed three *Jagdgruppen* with 100 Bf 109F fighters to ensure air superiority, five *Kampfgeschwader* with 134 Ju 88 and 34 He 111 bombers for battlefield interdiction and 67 Ju 87 Stuka dive-bombers from StG 77 for close air support. Two squadrons of reconnaissance aircraft were also provided for the vital tasks of directing the artillery and photographic reconnaissance. When Operation *Störfang* began on 2 June 1942, von Richthofen committed his fighters to conduct offensive counter-air operations over Sevastopol while bombers from KG 51 repeatedly attacked the Soviet airstrips, but these efforts failed to neutralize the Soviet fighter force. Initially, Oktyabrsky tried to conserve his fighters, but when the German ground attacks began on 7 June he committed them en masse. This was a mistake, since the large-scale air battles over Sevastopol during 7–13 June went against the Soviets, with losses of 47 aircraft. The Soviets immediately flew in the 45th Fighter Regiment from the Caucasus with 20 more Yak-1 fighters and thereafter avoided pitched battles. Despite German success in the opening fighter skirmishes, the Luftwaffe was unable to knock out the airstrips inside the Sevastopol perimeter and the Soviet fighters continued to fly missions from them until 30 June. German artillery shelled the Soviet airstrips, destroying a few aircraft on the ground, but also failed to shut down Soviet air operations. Furthermore, the small force of Il-2 and Pe-2 bombers available to Oktyabrsky was able to mount frequent low-level attacks on forward German units.

On 1 July, the remaining 31 Soviet aircraft flew out of Sevastopol to the Caucasus, giving complete air superiority to the Luftwaffe. During Operation *Störfang*, the Luftwaffe flew 23,751 sorties over Sevastopol, dropped 20,529 tons of bombs and destroyed 141 Soviet aircraft. Towards the end of *Störfang* Luftwaffe operations were hindered by shortages of fuel and bombs, as well as the withdrawal of part of Fliegerkorps VIII to support the main German summer offensive. At least 23 German aircraft were lost during the operation, mostly as a result of Soviet fighter interceptions.

AIR–SEA OPERATIONS 1941–42

The cardinal rule of siege operations is that the attacking force must prevent the defender from receiving supplies and reinforcements from outside. In this regard, the Germans failed miserably at Sevastopol because the Luftwaffe was unable to cut off the flow of food, ammunition and fresh replacements from the Caucasus into the Crimea. Furthermore, Operation *Barbarossa* neglected to make any provisions for naval operations in the Black Sea and this omission was continually to hinder Axis efforts to crush Soviet resistance first at Odessa, then at Sevastopol. Indeed, the Soviet Black Sea Fleet (Chernomorskiy Flot) provided capabilities that the Germans could never hope to match and at best, could only temporarily neutralize through the commitment of significant Luftwaffe resources.

German efforts to isolate Sevastopol began shortly after the onset of hostilities, when He 111s from II/KG 4 laid 120 magnetic mines off Sevastopol in June 1941. These mines succeeded in sinking the Soviet destroyer *Bystry*, but traffic into the port was only temporarily disrupted. After that, the Luftwaffe did not bother Sevastopol again until von Manstein's first offensive in November 1941. At that time, the handful of bombers and Stukas available were unable to impede the arrival of over 20,000 Soviet troops into Sevastopol by sea. The apparent weakness of the Luftwaffe in the Crimea in the fall of 1941 encouraged Oktyabrsky to retain a naval gunfire support unit in Sevastopol. The Luftwaffe units did achieve occasional successes, including the sinking off Yalta on 7 November of the transport *Armeniya* by KG 26's torpedo-carrying He 111s; about 5,000 Soviet wounded went down with the vessel. On 12 November, several Stukas from II/StG 77 caught the light cruiser *Chervona Ukraina* in the east end of Severnaya Bay and crippled it with three bomb hits. However, during von Manstein's December 1941 offensive, the long winter nights enabled the Black Sea Fleet to bring the battleship *Parizhskaya Kommuna* into Severnaya Bay to provide point-blank 12in. naval gunfire at the advancing German troops. By the end of the year, the Black Sea Fleet had brought over 48,000 troops into Sevastopol and evacuated over 2,200 wounded.

During the winter of 1941/42, the Luftwaffe continued to lay small numbers of magnetic mines off Sevastopol, which sank a few Soviet transports and another destroyer before Operation *Störfang* began. Despite the fact that the Soviets had little ability to sweep mines, the Luftwaffe failed to press this campaign aggressively, which could have seriously disrupted supply runs into Sevastopol. Despite constant Luftwaffe attacks, the Black Sea Fleet was able to bring over 35,000 reinforcements into Sevastopol in January–May 1942 and evacuate 9,000 wounded. The main weakness of the Black Sea Fleet was not vulnerability to the Luftwaffe but inadequate maintenance facilities after

The Soviet Black Sea Fleet had one battalion with 18 Maxim quadruple 7.62mm anti-aircraft machine guns for air defence. This weapon was too short ranged and could only provide limited protection for some of the coastal batteries. (Author's collection)

the loss of Nikolayev in August 1941 and Sevastopol became too dangerous for repairs. Forced to operate from minor ports in the Caucasus, by June 1942 the Black Sea Fleet had only two heavy cruisers, one light cruiser, eight destroyers and 24 submarines available to support the defence of Sevastopol. Even the battleship *Parizhskaya Kommuna* was unavailable, since its gun barrels were worn out after repeated firing in December 1941.

The Black Sea Fleet ran weekly supply convoys into Sevastopol from Novorossiysk, Tuapse and Poti. A typical convoy consisted of one or two destroyers, one or two small transport ships and a few minesweepers. Soviet warships did not have particularly strong anti-aircraft defences, but the Luftwaffe bombers and Stukas had great difficulty in hitting fast-moving ships. Captain 2nd Rank V. N. Eroshenko, commander of the flotilla leader *Tashkent*, made more runs into Sevastopol than any other ship, including six during Operation *Störfang*. The Soviets also used their large fleet of submarines to conduct 77 supply runs into Sevastopol in the period 7 May to 2 July, with three submarines lost.

By January 1942 the German OKH realized that the Luftwaffe alone could not blockade Sevastopol and it took steps to correct this. First, the Kriegsmarine was ordered to dispatch an S-Boat squadron with six boats to the Black Sea; this required dismantling the 92-ton boats and sending them down the Danube by barge to the Romanian port of Constanza on the Black Sea. However, the 1st S-Boat Flotilla under Kapitänleutnant Heinz Birnbacher was not ready to begin patrolling off Sevastopol until 17 June. The second option enacted by the OKH was a rare appeal to their Italian allies for help. Aware of the Italian expertise with light naval forces, the OKH requested the Italian Naval High Command to dispatch a light naval squadron to the Black Sea in time for the final attack on Sevastopol. The Regia Marina duly dispatched the 101st Squadron with four MAS motor torpedo boats, five explosive motorboats and six 'CB' class mini-submarines, under the command of the highly competent Capitano di Fregata Francesco Mimbelli. The 24-ton Italian MAS boats and 35-ton mini-submarines were easier to transport than the nearest German equivalents and they were moved by truck and barge to Romania. By mid-May 1942, the 101st Squadron was established in Yalta and Feodosiya, which made it the only Axis naval force available to support

The flotilla leader *Tashkent* carrying another load of troops into Sevastopol. The vessel had six 45mm anti-aircraft guns, which here are manned and ready, but its main defence against air attack was its capability to make high-speed dashes at up to 39 knots. (Author's collection)

Operation *Störfang*. The Italian MAS boats and mini-submarines quickly began to harass Soviet naval convoys into Sevastopol. However, the Italian light naval forces were vulnerable to Soviet air attack, and on 1 June 1942 von Manstein himself was nearly killed aboard an MAS boat that was strafed by two Yak-1 fighters from Sevastopol.

Although the Luftwaffe was heavily reinforced for Operation *Störfang*, it still could not sever Sevastopol's sea lines of communications. In June 1942, the Black Sea Fleet was able to transport over 18,000 reinforcements into Sevastopol, including the 138th and 142nd Naval Rifle Brigades. More than 11,000 wounded and civilians were evacuated in the same period. However, landing troops and supplies in Severnaya Bay did become more hazardous and German He 111 bombers were able to sink the destroyer *Svobodny* and the transport *Abkhaziya* in the bay on 10 June. On 18 June the flotilla leader *Kharkov* was badly damaged en route to Sevastopol and on 26 June Stukas sank the destroyer *Bezuprechny*. Birnbacher's S-Boats finally entered the battle on 17 June but missed two Soviet convoys in a row. Finally, on the night of 19 June the *S-27*, *S-72* and *S-102* attacked a convoy, sinking the small transport *Belostok* and damaging a minesweeper. However, between 23 and 25 June the S-Boats failed in three separate intercept attempts to stop Soviet convoys with the 142nd Naval Infantry Brigade from slipping into Sevastopol. The main effect of the S-Boat and MAS boat attacks was to induce greater caution on the part of Soviet convoy commanders, who feared night torpedo ambushes. In the final stages of *Störfang*, the light forces were partly shifted to other purposes, with the Italians used to make a feint landing near Cape Fiolent on the night of 28 June to distract the Soviet coastal defences from the actual crossing at Severnaya Bay. Birnbacher's S-Boats were used to screen the crossing of the German assault boats and prevent interference by Soviet light warships.

Captain Eroshenko made one last run into Sevastopol on 27 June, delivering over 900 troops and taking aboard 2,300 wounded and civilians. However, his destroyer was badly damaged by German bombers on the return trip and finally sunk at Novorossiysk on 2 July. The last Soviet resupply effort by sea into Sevastopol occurred on 28 June when two minesweepers brought in 330 troops.

The Luftwaffe's inability to conduct effective mining or anti-shipping operations off the Crimea proved to be the weak element of the Axis siege of Sevastopol. Sporadic successes could not conceal the fact that the bulk of Soviet convoys made it through virtually unscathed right up to the end of the siege, which enabled the garrison to hold out much longer. Intercepting the Soviet naval convoys proved far more difficult than the Axis leadership anticipated. In fact, the Soviet Black Sea Fleet displayed great courage, ingenuity and skill in keeping the sea lanes to Sevastopol open and the Axis naval interdiction efforts were far too little and too late to shift the balance against the overwhelming Soviet naval superiority.

OPERATION *STÖRFANG* – THE THIRD ASSAULT ON SEVASTOPOL

THE BOMBARDMENT BEGINS, 2 JUNE 1942

The Eleventh Army spent the last week of May shifting its forces back to Sevastopol, absorbing replacements and re-stocking its ammunition reserves. Von Manstein intended to precede his final assault upon Sevastopol with a five-day air and artillery bombardment to weaken the Soviet defences, and this artillery preparation began at 0540hrs on 2 June, with a few select battalions such as the 737th Artillery Battalion using its Czech-made 149mm s.FH 37 howitzers to conduct long-range harassing fires. Twenty minutes later, the bombardment began in earnest with most of the division-level 105mm and 150mm howitzers firing battalion-sized three-round missions against identified targets in the Soviet main defensive belts. Battalion-level 81mm mortars and regimental-level 75mm and 150mm infantry guns engaged Soviet forward infantry positions. The German artillery preparation was methodical rather than overwhelming, pausing to assess damage and adjust fire onto subsequent targets. The 306th Army Artillery Command had divided the Soviet defensive zones into boxes, with each identified bunker or trench given a number, and the artillery planned to sweep each box over the course of the five-day bombardment. LIV Corps had the 31st and 556th Artillery Observation Battalions, while XXX Corps had the 29th Observation Battalion, all of which

A German artillery *Unteroffizier* in one of the forward observation posts. The Eleventh Army had three artillery observation battalions who methodically mapped out all the front-line Soviet positions prior to the offensive. (Nik Cornish, WH106)

A German 150mm s.FH 18 howitzer crew preparing to ram the shell in the tube. The Eleventh Army had 21 batteries with 81 s.FH 18 howitzers at Sevastopol. This weapon could fire a 43kg high explosive shell out to a maximum of 13,250m and was the primary element of the medium German artillery. (Nik Cornish Archive, WH387)

used sound-flash platoons to identify and locate any Soviet artillery units that fired in response to the bombardment. The heavier German corps-level guns waited until about 1100hrs before joining in, although only 22 rounds of 420mm and 62 rounds of 305mm were fired on the first day. By midday the German artillerymen switched to 'destruction fire' against major enemy strongpoints, typically firing a battalion-sized two-round mission from a 210mm mortar or 240mm howitzer unit. The German fire on the first day apparently did little harm to the Soviet defences, and Petrov withheld most of his artillery from responding. By 1650hrs the German fire began to subside with only 362 tons of ammunition used on the first day. Most of the German divisional-level howitzers had fired 6–12 rounds on 2 June, saving themselves and their ammunition for the main event.

Luftwaffe operations began at 0600hrs on 2 June, with the Ju 87 Stukas of StG 77 and bombers of KG 76 and KG 100 dropping 570 tons of bombs, including one 1,700kg and seven 1,400kg concrete-piercing bombs. The Stukas were tasked to attack point targets, such as individual forts and bunkers, while the level-bombers were directed to attack area targets, including enemy reserves, artillery positions and the harbour area. Most of the Luftwaffe attacks were directed against the Soviet Defensive Sector IV, with less support for XXX Corps. Although German fighters continuously attacked the Soviet airfields south-west of Sevastopol, they were unable to completely shut down Soviet defensive fighter missions. Even worse, the Luftwaffe failed to stop a convoy from Tuapse comprising the flotilla leader *Tashkent*, destroyer *Bezuprechny*, a transport, the 836-ton tanker *Mikhail Gromov* and six small auxiliaries from reaching Sevastopol on the evening of 2 June. Twelve He 111s from II/KG 26 attacked the convoy and sank the tanker, but the rest of the ships reached their destination and delivered ammunition and 2,785 troops.

COUNTDOWN TO X-DAY, 3–6 JUNE 1942

The German bombardment continued over the next four days, usually beginning in earnest between 0300–0320hrs when visibility permitted clear observation of the targets. Each day, the weight of fire increased as more

Soviet defences in Sevastopol, 2 June 1942

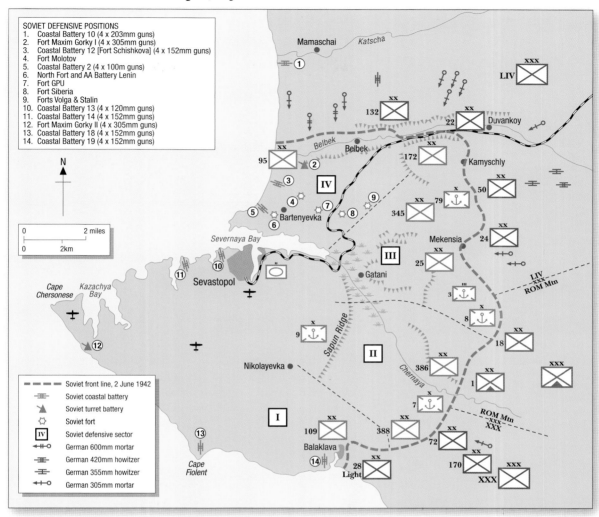

SOVIET DEFENSIVE POSITIONS
1. Coastal Battery 10 (4 x 203mm guns)
2. Fort Maxim Gorky I (4 x 305mm guns)
3. Coastal Battery 12 [Fort Schishkova] (4 x 152mm guns)
4. Fort Molotov
5. Coastal Battery 2 (4 x 100m guns)
6. North Fort and AA Battery Lenin
7. Fort GPU
8. Fort Siberia
9. Forts Volga & Stalin
10. Coastal Battery 13 (4 x 120mm guns)
11. Coastal Battery 14 (4 x 152mm guns)
12. Fort Maxim Gorky II (4 x 305mm guns)
13. Coastal Battery 18 (4 x 152mm guns)
14. Coastal Battery 19 (4 x 152mm guns)

N

| 0 | 2 miles |
| 0 | 2km |

Soviet front line, 2 June 1942
Soviet coastal battery
Soviet turret battery
Soviet fort
IV   Soviet defensive sector
German 600mm mortar
German 420mm howitzer
German 355mm howitzer
German 305mm mortar

batteries joined the bombardment. Typical targets were individual timber or earth bunkers, which usually received 10–25 rounds each of 105mm fire; 210mm mortars usually targeted concrete bunkers. The Eleventh Army was also very aggressive about moving its 88mm Flak guns up to the front to fire directly into the apertures of bunkers, while the much-maligned 37mm Pak 36 anti-tank did splendid work engaging machine-gun bunkers with the new Stielgranate 41 hollow-charge shell.

The 306th Army Artillery Command concentrated its heaviest weapons against the main Soviet defensive positions along the Belbek River and the Kamyschly Ravine. The Ölberg, a key hilltop position that guarded the main rail line into Sevastopol, was hit by 30 rounds from the 420mm Gamma mortar on 4 June as well as numerous 305mm mortar rounds. The Eisenbahnberg, another important hill position, was hit by 20 420mm Gamma rounds, 30 305mm rounds and 40 280mm howitzer shells. Haccius Ridge was worked over repeatedly by the 105mm and 150mm howitzers of the 132nd Infantry Division, as well as at least 50 rounds from 280mm

One of the two 600mm Karl mortars from the 833rd Heavy Artillery Battalion being loaded with a 2.1-ton concrete-piercing shell from its ammunition carrier. The converted PzKpfw IV chassis could carry four shells and each Karl had two such carriers. (HITM Photo Research)

howitzers. Considerable attention was also given to the suspected Soviet reserve and artillery positions around the Mekenziyevy Mountain train station, including repeated Stuka and bomber attacks. Despite the weight of metal thrown at them, Soviet casualties in the five-day preparation phase were far from crippling; the 514th Rifle Regiment reported 12 killed and 20 wounded, while one company from the 79th Naval Infantry Brigade suffered 16 casualties among its 78 men.

Between 2 and 6 June, the Eleventh Army fired a total of 42,595 rounds equivalent to 2,449 tons of munitions. Some nine per cent of Eleventh Army's ammunition stockpile was expended in the preparation phase. German divisional artillery fired 19,750 rounds of 105mm and 5,300 rounds of 150mm ammunition in the five-day bombardment. Infantry guns fired another 4,200 rounds of 75mm and 150mm ammunition, plus 5,300 81mm mortar rounds. The corps-level *Nebelwerfer* battalions remained silent during this phase, not firing a single rocket. Two-thirds of the super heavy artillery rounds fired in the prep phase were from the four 240mm H39 howitzers and 16 305mm Skoda mortars.

The heaviest weapons, the Karl mortars and 'Dora', only played a minor role in the opening bombardment. One Karl mortar fired two registration rounds on 2 June, but the battalion then was not committed until 6 June. After an immense engineering effort, 'Dora' was finally installed at Bakhchysaray 25km north-east of Sevastopol and was ready for firing on 5 June. At 0535hrs, 'Dora' fired one of its 7-ton shells at Fort Maxim Gorky I's Bastion I, and then proceeded to lob eight rounds at the minor Coastal Battery 2 near the harbour entrance. Accuracy was poor, with most rounds missing by 300m or more. Six rounds were then fired at Fort Stalin, with the closest round landing within 35–40m of the target and most impacting 130–260m away. On 6 June, 'Dora' opened fire in the evening and fired seven rounds at Fort Molotov; one round struck within 80m of the target, three rounds within 165–210m, one round within 310m, one round 500m off and one round 615m off. 'Dora' was then directed against a cleverly camouflaged ammunition dump named White Cliff on the northern side of Severnaya Bay and fired nine rounds with no effect.

It was more difficult for the Germans to employ the clumsy and short-range Karl system, but on the late afternoon of 6 June the men of the 1st Battery/833rd Heavy Artillery Battalion were able to manoeuvre the 600mm mortar known as 'Thor' up onto a hill just 1,200m from the nearest Soviet positions of the 95th Rifle Division. From this location, 'Thor' had a clear line of sight to Fort Maxim Gorky I 3,700m to the south, and at 1700hrs it started lobbing 16 of its 2-ton concrete-piercing shells at the target. One of the shells hit Turret No. 2, severely damaging the weapon and causing casualties among the crew. 'Thor' was less effective against Bastion I, which contained the fort's communications and range-finding equipment, but a Stuka attack succeeded in knocking out the cable trunk. All told, Coastal Battery 30 suffered about 40 casualties among its 290 naval gunners during the air and artillery bombardment, but neither 'Thor' nor 'Dora' had succeeded in destroying the installation.

Although the use of super-heavy weapons such as the Karl mortars and 'Dora' may have undermined the morale of the Soviet troops on the receiving end of multi-ton shells, these weapons actually failed to make a significant contribution commensurate with their cost. Primary responsibility must rest with General der Artillerie Zuckertort, the commander of the 306th Army Artillery Command, who violated the cardinal rule of artillery support in that he allowed these expensive weapons to fire too few rounds at too many targets, resulting in none of them actually being destroyed. 'Dora' had only 48 rounds available but Zuckertort used them against eight different targets, including only nine rounds against the primary target of Fort Maxim Gorky I. Furthermore, the super-heavy artillery of 420mm or larger all ran out of ammunition early in the offensive and it was the less-celebrated Czech-made 305mm mortars and 240mm howitzers that made the greater contribution and continued to fire from the first day of the offensive to the last.

The main target for the Karl mortars, as well as 'Dora' and the 420mm Gamma mortar was the Soviet-held Bastion I. This was the heavily fortified fire-direction centre for Coastal Battery 30 (Fort Maxim Gorky I). (NARA)

The Luftwaffe also continued to pound the Soviet defences during the period 3–6 June, dropping a total of 1,694 tons of bombs. Since almost all the bombers were based within 50–60km of Sevastopol, they could make multiple sorties per day. Coastal Battery 14 on the west side of Sevastopol was hit by bombers on 3 June, destroying one of its four 152mm guns but otherwise the coastal batteries proved to be very difficult targets to destroy. Furthermore, the Luftwaffe failed again to prevent the Black Sea Fleet from bringing 2,551 more troops into Sevastopol during 3–6 June. Meanwhile, the Soviet 3rd OAG continued to contest the skies over Sevastopol with 50–60 sorties per day. The Soviets held back most of their artillery during the period 2–6 June

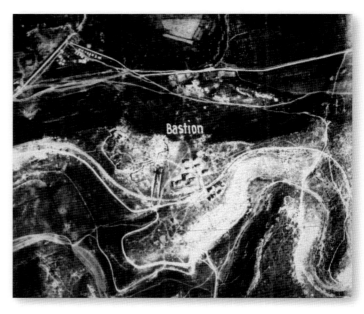

because of limited ammunition supplies and concern about exposing their few heavy weapons to enemy counterbattery fire or Stuka attack. At the start of June, the SOR had about 200–300 rounds for each of its howitzers and 600–700 rounds for each mortar. Yet Soviet observers were vigilant and when they could confirm the location of a German artillery unit, they would call upon a few designated 'sniper batteries' that could shoot and then re-position. During the period 2–6 June, the Soviets destroyed three German artillery pieces, including a precious 280mm howitzer.

XXX CORPS AND ROMANIAN MOUNTAIN CORPS, 2–7 JUNE

In contrast to the firepower placed at the disposal of Hansen's LIV Corps, Fretter-Pico's XXX Corps in the south and the Romanian Mountain Corps in the centre were given only modest artillery and air support. Martinek, who directed the 110th Army Artillery Command's corps artillery as well as the divisional artillery units, started the bombardment with a total of only 171 guns and 36 rocket launchers in 18 battalions. Furthermore, most of Martinek's assets were lighter 105mm pieces, including two battalions of Romanian guns and two battalions of elderly German pieces from

Table: German Eleventh Army expenditure of heavy artillery ammunition, 2–20 June 1942. *(Red means out of ammunition.)*

Super-Heavy Artillery (Rounds Fired)									
Date	Total ammunition expended (tons)	800mm 'Dora'	600mm Karl	420mm	355mm	305mm	283mm 'Long Bruno'	280mm	240mm
2-Jun-42	362		2	52		62	104	330	138
3-Jun-42	445					105			20
4-Jun-42	467					73			40
5-Jun-42	538	9		30		183			163
6-Jun-42	637	16	16	1	25	163			204
7-Jun-42	3,939	13	54	26	34	460	32	410	480
8-Jun-42	1,661				15	207	48	190	160
9-Jun-42	1,805		50	36	31	304	40	296	305
10-Jun-42	596		(out)	17	32	132	58	280	100
11-Jun-42	2,561	5	(out)	81	22	272	44	252	22
12-Jun-42	2,444		(out)	26	38	679	41	293	
13-Jun-42	2,311		(out)	7	61	503	39	169	70
14-Jun-42	1,995		(out)	(out)	8	264	34	101	74
15-Jun-42	1,477		(out)	(out)	6	186	40	90	85
16-Jun-42	2,080		(out)	(out)	13	109	40	90	25
17-Jun-42	2,746	5	(out)	(out)	28	258	37	182	51
18-Jun-42	2,168	(out)	(out)	(out)	9	99	65	2	94
19-Jun-42	1,271	(out)	(out)	(out)	20	44	66	10	60
20-Jun-42	1,055	(out)	(out)	(out)		45	22		

A Soviet-held hill in XXX Corps sector under heavy artillery bombardment. The German artillery plan called for firing a few large-calibre rounds at a specific target – such as a bunker – then pausing to assess results. Note that some earlier rounds have already set vegetation afire, causing smoke that could obscure observation. (Anne S. K. Brown)

World War I. Heavy artillery support was limited to a single battery with two Czech-made 305mm mortars and two batteries of 240mm howitzers, as well as two batteries with three modern 150mm K 39 guns that had a maximum range of over 24km.

Von Manstein had decided that XXX Corps would not conduct any major ground attacks until at least the day after the beginning of the LIV Corps attack, so that Fliegerkorps VIII could provide the bulk of its sorties to supporting his main effort. Given a supporting role, Fretter-Pico intended to gradually chip away at the outermost layer of Soviet fortified positions with small-scale infantry–artillery assaults rather than to try to achieve a quick breakthrough as Hansen attempted. Unlike Zuckertort's grand barrage for LIV Corps, Martinek used his artillery sparingly during 2–7 June to target known Soviet artillery positions primarily around Kadykovka, Fort Kuppe and Chapel Hill. Soviet counterbattery fire inflicted over 100 casualties upon XXX Corps in this period, plus the loss of one 105mm l.FH 18 howitzer. On Fretter-Pico's flank, the Romanian Mountain Corps committed only a few of its batteries to the initial bombardment.

Fretter-Pico decided to make his first move on the corps' left flank, hoping to push the Soviets off the high ground east of Balaklava. At 0400hrs on the morning of 7 June – following a 15-minute artillery preparation – III/49th Jäger Regiment from the 28th Light Division infiltrated into low ground between the Vermilion I and II hilltops, held by the Soviet 2nd Battalion/381st Rifle Regiment. The *Jäger* were able to get some men atop the small hills but were soon driven off by mortar and machine-gun fire. However, part of the *Jäger* battalion was able to slip past the main Soviet positions and moved onto Vermilion III, where it promptly began to dig in. A Soviet counterattack on this exposed unit was quickly driven off, but the position was precarious. At 0420hrs, a single battalion of the 83rd Jäger Regiment attacked the Soviet 456th NKVD Regiment's fortified position on the Sulzbacher Hill. Despite the concentrated artillery fire, the 456th NKVD Regiment was a tough, disciplined unit that held its ground. The Soviet troops repulsed the *Jäger* by firing flak guns at them in direct fire mode. Nevertheless, the men from the 83rd Jäger Regiment succeeded in occupying a small, fortified hillock near a

A Skoda 305mm M17 L/12 mortar. Although originally designed in 1908, this weapon was so useful in destroying bunkers that Germany kept it in production until 1943. The Eleventh Army had 16 of these ex-Austrian mortars and they fired 4,922 rounds during the final offensive. (Nik Cornish Archive, WH846)

wine vineyard known as Weingut, thereby strengthening the hold on the nearby Vermilion III. General-Major Novikov's 109th Rifle Division reacted to these small advances with a series of violent counterattacks and constant mortar barrages that reduced one German *Jäger* company on Vermilion III from 70 men to 20, and another company to 30. Novikov's riflemen kept attacking in small groups during the night and gradually pushed the *Jäger* off both captured positions. By midnight, XXX Corps had suffered 500 casualties and was pushed back to its start line. Soviet counterbattery fire had been particularly effective, destroying a battery of four 150mm *Nebelwerfer* and a Czech-made 149mm s.FHM 37(t) howitzer.

While the 28th Light Division was probing on XXX Corps' left flank, the Romanian 1st Mountain Division made several attempts to seize Sugar Loaf and North Nose on the corps' right flank. Despite support from XXX Corps artillery, the Romanians failed to make any progress and were easily repulsed by the Soviet 769th Rifle Regiment. Fretter-Pico's opening move was far too puny and unimaginative considering that the Soviets had over six months to fortify these positions. Von Manstein was disappointed by the losses suffered by XXX Corps for negligible gains and ordered Fretter-Pico not to commit his forces in piecemeal fashion again.

7 JUNE 1942, X-DAY

After five days of bombardment, the Soviets expected an imminent ground assault. On the evening of 6 June around 2300hrs, Soviet artillery supporting Defensive Sectors III and IV began shooting harassing fires against suspected German troop assembly areas. In spite of this, at 0315hrs the 306th Army Artillery Command began a massive one-hour 'destruction fire', concentrating on the area between Haccius Ridge and Trapez. Both 'Odin' and 'Thor' joined the bombardment, firing a total of 54 rounds against Coastal Battery 30's turrets and Bastion I, as well as against targets around Belbek. Infantry guns and mortars fired for effect against the front-line trenches in the Belbek Valley, while *Nebelwerfer* hit the second-line positions and 305mm mortars worked over key targets such as the Ölberg. Unlike the previous five days, the German artillery fired at nearly maximum rates of fire and did not pause to assess damage. The effect on the forward Soviet positions around the Stellenberg (Hill 124) was stunning as infantry fighting positions were pounded mercilessly. Long-range guns went after targets in the Soviet rear, particularly reserves and known artillery positions. The Soviet 7th Naval Infantry Brigade, sitting in reserve well behind the line, was particularly hard hit and lost most of the 200 replacements that had just arrived to a combined air and artillery attack. However, 'Dora' continued to waste rounds firing against the White Cliff ammunition dump – which prompted an angry rebuke directly from Hitler to stop misusing the weapon against such targets. Although the Germans claimed that 'Dora' destroyed the dump – a claim that may be exaggerated – it is clear that it had failed to neutralize Fort Maxim Gorky I, which continued to fire periodically throughout 7 June.

Even before the German artillery barrage paused, infantry from the 132nd Infantry Division's 436th Infantry Regiment began to work their way southwards towards the Belbek River. At 0425hrs, LIV Corps' main effort – Generalmajor Ludwig Wolff's 22nd Infantry Division – began its attack with all three of its infantry regiments on line heading south-west towards the Ölberg. In the path of the oncoming 16th and 47th Infantry Regiments was Hill 124, known as the Stellenberg to the Germans. Hill 124 had been steadily pounded for five days and the Soviet 2nd/79th Naval Infantry Brigade had reduced its garrison to only the 5th Company, while keeping its other two companies farther back in reserve. The bombardment had shaken the 5th Company badly and the Soviets did not have a chance to get their reserves up to Hill 124 before the first assault groups from the 16th and 47th Infantry Regiments arrived. The Germans did have to cross a dense anti-personnel minefield in front of Hill 124, giving the defenders a chance to recover and begin placing machine-gun fire on the German infantry. However, the German assault groups had well rehearsed this part of the attack and they were soon through the wire and the mines and the isolated 5th Company was hit by two battalions worth of Germans nearly simultaneously. The 5th Company fought well but soon crumbled under the concentric attack and the handful of survivors fled back to the reserve positions. Generalmajor Wolff ordered his regiments to continue the attack and the I/47th Infantry Regiment under Major Gustav Alvermann succeeded in slipping through a gap in the mines south of the Stellenberg and seized the Soviet 79th Naval Infantry Brigade's reserve positions near the Eisenbahnberg at 0815hrs. Alvermann,

Another new artillery piece was the 150mm K- 39 heavy gun, seen here in marching order with the barrel mounted on its transporter. The 1st Battery, 767th Artillery Battalion, had three of these guns and 2,700 rounds at the start of the offensive to support the 24th and 50th Infantry Divisions. The K- 39, originally built for export to Turkey but taken over by the Wehrmacht in 1939, had a maximum range of 25.4km. (HITM Photo Research)

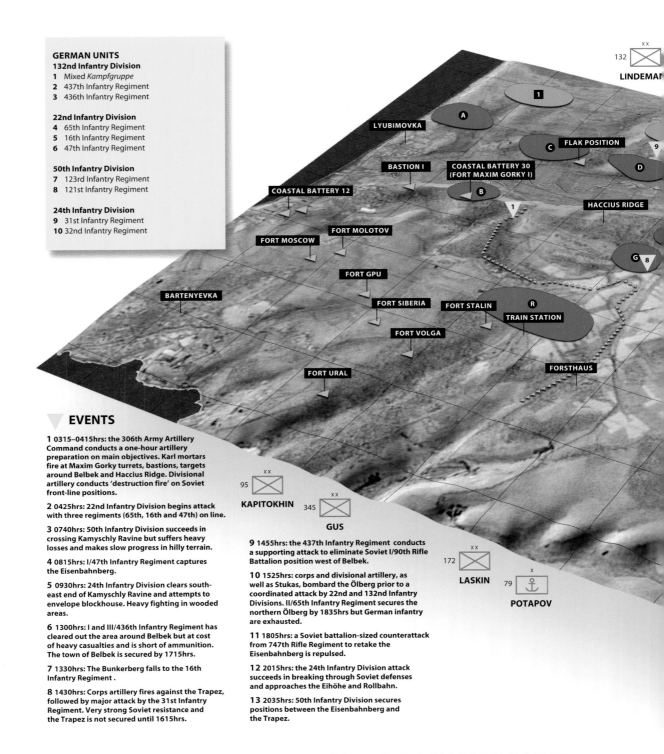

GERMAN UNITS

132nd Infantry Division
1 Mixed *Kampfgruppe*
2 437th Infantry Regiment
3 436th Infantry Regiment

22nd Infantry Division
4 65th Infantry Regiment
5 16th Infantry Regiment
6 47th Infantry Regiment

50th Infantry Division
7 123rd Infantry Regiment
8 121st Infantry Regiment

24th Infantry Division
9 31st Infantry Regiment
10 32nd Infantry Regiment

132 LINDEMA[N]

LYUBIMOVKA

A
1
C FLAK POSITION
D
9

BASTION I
COASTAL BATTERY 30 (FORT MAXIM GORKY I)
COASTAL BATTERY 12
B
1
HACCIUS RIDGE

FORT MOLOTOV
FORT MOSCOW
G 8

FORT GPU

BARTENYEVKA
FORT SIBERIA FORT STALIN
R
TRAIN STATION

FORT VOLGA

FORT URAL
FORSTHAUS

EVENTS

1 0315–0415hrs: the 306th Army Artillery Command conducts a one-hour artillery preparation on main objectives. Karl mortars fire at Maxim Gorky turrets, bastions, targets around Belbek and Haccius Ridge. Divisional artillery conducts 'destruction fire' on Soviet front-line positions.

2 0425hrs: 22nd Infantry Division begins attack with three regiments (65th, 16th and 47th) on line.

3 0740hrs: 50th Infantry Division succeeds in crossing Kamyschly Ravine but suffers heavy losses and makes slow progress in hilly terrain.

4 0815hrs: I/47th Infantry Regiment captures the Eisenbahnberg.

5 0930hrs: 24th Infantry Division clears southeast end of Kamyschly Ravine and attempts to envelope blockhouse. Heavy fighting in wooded areas.

6 1300hrs: I and III/436th Infantry Regiment has cleared out the area around Belbek but at cost of heavy casualties and is short of ammunition. The town of Belbek is secured by 1715hrs.

7 1330hrs: The Bunkerberg falls to the 16th Infantry Regiment .

8 1430hrs: Corps artillery fires against the Trapez, followed by major attack by the 31st Infantry Regiment. Very strong Soviet resistance and the Trapez is not secured until 1615hrs.

95 KAPITOKHIN 345 GUS

9 1455hrs: the 437th Infantry Regiment conducts a supporting attack to eliminate Soviet I/90th Rifle Battalion position west of Belbek.

10 1525hrs: corps and divisional artillery, as well as Stukas, bombard the Ölberg prior to a coordinated attack by 22nd and 132nd Infantry Divisions. II/65th Infantry Regiment secures the northern Ölberg by 1835hrs but German infantry are exhausted.

11 1805hrs: a Soviet battalion-sized counterattack from 747th Rifle Regiment to retake the Eisenbahnberg is repulsed.

12 2015hrs: the 24th Infantry Division attack succeeds in breaking through Soviet defenses and approaches the Eihöhe and Rollbahn.

13 2035hrs: 50th Infantry Division secures positions between the Eisenbahnberg and the Trapez.

172 LASKIN 79 POTAPOV

INITIAL GROUND ATTACK OF THE GERMAN LIV CORPS ON X-DAY, 7 JUNE 1942

Vieed from the south showing the attack of the German LIV Corps to clear the Soviet outer defenses on the north side of Severnaya Bay. The main attack occurs across the Kamyschly Ravine.

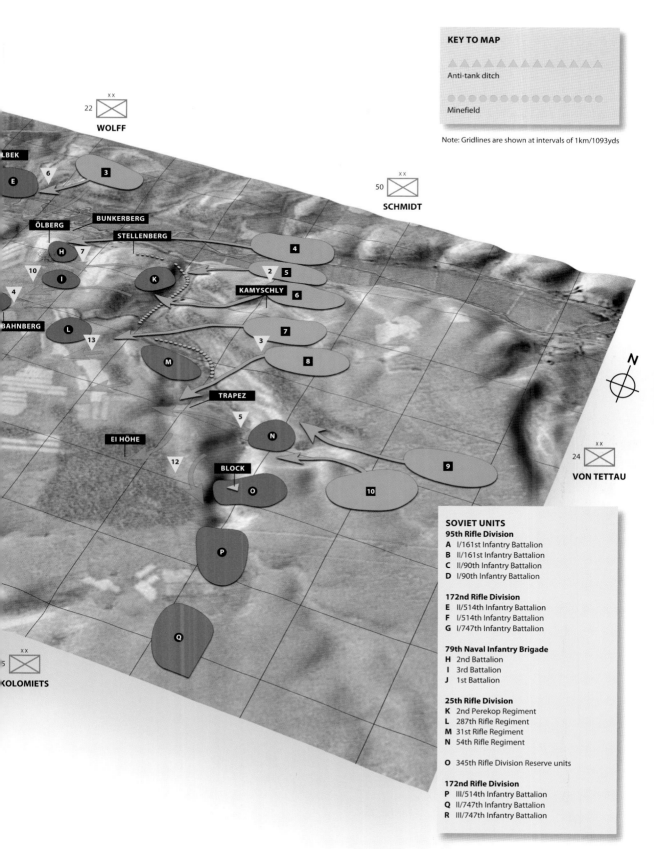

KEY TO MAP

▲▲▲▲▲▲▲▲▲▲▲▲▲▲

Anti-tank ditch

●●●●●●●●●●●●●●●●

Minefield

Note: Gridlines are shown at intervals of 1km/1093yds

22 ⊠ × ×
WOLFF

50 ⊠ × ×
SCHMIDT

24 ⊠ × ×
VON TETTAU

⊠ × ×
KOLOMIETS

LBEK

E   6   3

ÖLBERG   BUNKERBERG

STELLENBERG

H   7

10   I   4   K   2   5   4

KAMYSCHLY   6

BAHNBERG   L   13   3   7

M   8

TRAPEZ

EI HÖHE   5   N   9

12   BLOCK   10

O

P

Q

N

SOVIET UNITS

95th Rifle Division
A   I/161st Infantry Battalion
B   II/161st Infantry Battalion
C   II/90th Infantry Battalion
D   I/90th Infantry Battalion

172nd Rifle Division
E   II/514th Infantry Battalion
F   I/514th Infantry Battalion
G   I/747th Infantry Battalion

79th Naval Infantry Brigade
H   2nd Battalion
I   3rd Battalion
J   1st Battalion

25th Rifle Division
K   2nd Perekop Regiment
L   287th Rifle Regiment
M   31st Rifle Regiment
N   54th Rifle Regiment

O   345th Rifle Division Reserve units

172nd Rifle Division
P   III/514th Infantry Battalion
Q   II/747th Infantry Battalion
R   III/747th Infantry Battalion

A German aerial photo of the Kamyschly Ravine, taken on 19 April 1942. Soviet defensive trenches on the Stellenberg are on the left and marked in white. This area was held by the Soviet 2nd Battalion of the 79th Naval Infantry Brigade and was the main attack sector for the German 22nd Infantry Division on 7 June 1942. (NARA)

who had won the Knight's Cross for his role in the assault on Valkenburg Airfield in Holland in May 1940, was killed during the fighting on the Eisenbahnberg. Meanwhile on the left flank of LIV Corps, the 50th and 24th Infantry Divisions launched supporting attacks with two regiments each across the Kamyschly Ravine between 0740hrs and 0930hrs. The artillery preparation had been less effective in this area and the steep slopes and wooded terrain made for very slow going, particularly for the assault guns. In short order, Soviet anti-tank guns knocked out four of 12 assault guns and the attack bogged down. Efforts to use B IV remote-control demolition vehicles failed owing to the hilly terrain.

The 22nd Infantry Division continued its slow drive towards the Ölberg, with its 16th Infantry Regiment capturing Hill 126 – known as the Bunkerberg to the Germans – at 1330hrs after tough fighting. The Bunkerberg had been held by a battalion of the 747th Rifle Regiment of the 172nd Rifle Division, and this represented the boundary between the 172nd Rifle Division and the 79th Naval Infantry Brigade, as well as the boundary between the Soviet Defensive Sectors III and IV. The *Schwerpunkt* of LIV Corps' attack was aimed at this seam and Hansen now ordered the 22nd Infantry Division to prepare for a coordinated assault upon the Ölberg after a major air and artillery bombardment. The 132nd Infantry Division, still mopping up around Belbek, was ordered to support the attack on the Ölberg from the north. The 306th Army Artillery Command fired a concentrated barrage against the Trapez position (Hill 195) at 1430hrs, since this position had been holding up the 50th Infantry Division's ability to cover the left flank of the main effort. After heavy fighting, the Trapez was secured at 1615hrs. The main attack on the Ölberg began at 1525hrs with a massed Stuka attack and the bombardment of most of the corps' artillery. While the 16th Infantry Regiment tried to move against the Ölberg's eastern flank, II/165th Infantry

Regiment was able to infiltrate from the north and succeeded in securing the northern slope of the objective. However, the German infantry was exhausted and the Soviet 3rd/514th Rifle Regiment would not budge. By 1835hrs the Germans had succeeded in seizing part of the Ölberg, but the attack was spent. On the left flank of LIV Corps, the 24th Infantry Division had finally achieved a major breakthrough late in the day, advancing towards the Eihöhe (Hill 205.7) at 2015hrs and nearly encircling the 287th Rifle Regiment. On the corps' right flank, the 132nd Infantry Division had gradually cleared the area around Belbek Village and was beginning to push in the 95th Rifle Division's forward positions.

Throughout the day, the Soviets had counterattacked with mortars, artillery and aircraft. The mortar fire from the 25th Rifle Division had been particularly heavy against the 50th and 24th Infantry Divisions in the Kamyschly Ravine, causing significant casualties. Meanwhile, Soviet pilots had launched three major air strikes against the 22nd Infantry Division's positions around the Stellenberg and near the Ölberg. The only significant Soviet ground counterattack on 7 June was a battalion-sized assault from the 747th Rifle Regiment's reserve battalion in an attempt to retake the Eisenbahnberg from the 16th Infantry Regiment at 1805hrs, but this was easily repulsed.

German losses in LIV Corps on X-Day had been serious, with at least 2,357 casualties in the four assault divisions, including 340 killed. The 1st and 3rd Battalions of the 47th Infantry Regiment were particularly hard hit by the fighting around the Eisenbahnberg. The corps had also expended a prodigious amount of ammunition – some 3,939 tons worth – and the 132nd Infantry Division had used virtually its entire basic load of ammunition by midday. Although LIV Corps had not succeeded in breaking through the outer defences, the main effort had advanced over 2km through dense concentrations of mines and bunkers. The Soviet defenders had also suffered serious losses, with at least three battalions effectively destroyed. A number of individual Soviet fighting positions and small bunkers that had been bypassed during the day continued to harass the Germans around the Stellenberg, until they were gradually silenced. For the Soviets, the fact that the formidable obstacle of the Kamyschly Ravine had been overcome so quickly was a foreboding sign that the attackers were gaining the upper hand.

BELOW LEFT
A Soviet anti-aircraft crew loads a round into an 85mm KS-12 AA gun as the gun leader points at an aerial target. About 160 76mm and 85mm guns protected Sevastopol. After most of the guns in open mounts such as this one were destroyed by German artillery fire, the Soviets began hiding the remaining guns in fake warehouses near the bay and other concealed positions. (Central Museum of the Armed Forces, Moscow)

BELOW RIGHT
The Eleventh Army had a single unit, the 502nd Battery, with three of the new 170mm Kanone 18 heavy guns. This gun could fire a 68kg shell up to 28km, although the battery had only 153 rounds available at the start of the offensive. These weapons were deployed individually in support of the 22nd Infantry Division's attack across the Kamyschly Ravine. (HITM Photo Research)

COUNTERATTACK BY THE SOVIET 79TH NAVAL INFANTRY BRIGADE AGAINST THE GERMAN 50TH INFANTRY DIVISION NEAR THE FORSTHAUS, 11 JUNE 1942

On 10 June 1942, the German LIV Corps was able to capture the Mekenziyevy Mountain train station and a nearby road junction known as the Forsthaus (Mekenei No. 1 to the Soviets), thereby pushing a dangerous salient between the Soviet Defensive Sectors III and IV. However, the left flank of the salient, held by the German 50th Infantry Division, appeared to be thinly held. On the morning of 11 June, Polkovnik A. S. Potapov's 79th Naval Infantry Brigade was ordered to launch a counterattack into the flank of the 50th Infantry Division, in order to weaken the German hold on the Forsthaus. The counterattack was spearheaded by the 1st and 2nd Battalions, each down to about 50 per cent strength in their infantry companies. Although Petrov attempted to provide for extensive fire support from the 134th and 265th Artillery Regiments, the destroyer *Bditelny* and the armoured train 'Zhelezniakov', the plan fell apart because of the 79th Naval Infantry Brigade's last-minute efforts to coordinate with limited means of communication. Nevertheless, the black-clad sailors advanced toward the German outpost line, which proved to be thinly held in this area.

The Germans usually posted MG34 teams in hastily fortified shell craters or captured Soviet trenches, backed up by an infantry squad, to serve as their forward combat outposts.

This tactic allowed most of their infantry to rest and reorganize for the next assault, but left the front line vulnerable to sudden Soviet counterattacks.

In this scene, a platoon of naval infantrymen has eliminated a German MG34 position with hand grenades and is advancing past it. Many of the naval infantrymen are armed with the excellent SVT-40 semi-automatic rifle (1), which is far superior to the German bolt-action K98k rifle. Each squad has a 7.62mm DP light machine gun (2) and about 15 per cent of the troops are armed with the superb PPSch-41 sub-machine gun (3). Although the Soviets took some German prisoners (4) on the battlefield at Sevastopol, most were probably shot soon after interrogation. The 79th Naval Infantry Brigade was able to penetrate the German outpost line and advance 600m, but once it reached the main line of resistance of the 50th Division it was stopped cold by massed artillery fires and the StuG IIIs of the 190th Assault Gun Battalion. Stukas were also called in and they began to drop anti-personnel bombs on the exposed Soviet attackers. Caught in the open, the sailors suffered heavy losses and were forced back to their start line. Despite the lack of success, the morale of the Soviet naval infantrymen never cracked and they continued to counterattack until their units were completely burnt out.

THE BATTLE OF ATTRITION, 8–12 JUNE 1942

Hansen's LIV Corps had broken through the outer crust of the Soviet defence near the seam of Defensive Sectors III and IV on the first day and the Germans intended to push their advantage before Petrov could repair the damage to his lines. However, the Soviets struck first with a weak counterattack by the 1st Battalion/2nd Perekop Regiment and six T-26 light tanks from the 81st Tank Battalion against II/32nd Infantry Regiment near the Eihöhe, in an effort to relieve pressure on the nearly encircled 287th Rifle Regiment. The Soviet counterattack failed because of poor coordination between tanks, infantry and artillery. At 1000hrs, after a 30-minute artillery preparation by the 306th Army Artillery Command, LIV Corps resumed its attacks with the main *Schwerpunkt* now a coordinated drive on the Mekenziyevy Mountain railway station by the 22nd and 132nd Infantry Divisions. The 132nd Infantry Division was able to clear out the 'Ölberg' and most of the Haccius Ridge with its 437th Infantry Regiment driving westward, while its 436th Infantry Regiment advanced nearly 2km south-west of the Ölberg. Meanwhile, Wolff's 22nd Infantry Division advanced over 1km to the south-west from the Eisenbahnberg and overran much of the 79th Naval Infantry Brigade in the process. The Soviets still held the train station with the 383rd Rifle Regiment and the adjacent fortified position known as the Forsthaus with the remnants of the 79th Naval Infantry Brigade, but Petrov had few reserves to bolster his depleted front-line units. A single battalion, the 1st Battalion/241st Rifle Regiment, was hastily marched up to block the 132nd Infantry Division from outflanking Fort Maxim Gorky I. Throughout the day, Petrov was handicapped by poor communications that made it difficult for him to assess the extent of German advances, as well as incessant air attacks that made it difficult to move reserves forward during daylight. Hansen's LIV Corps suffered more than 1,700 casualties on 8 June but had created a lodgement that was 3km deep and 5km wide in Sevastopol's outer defensive ring.

On 9 June, LIV Corps continued to slowly grind forward in the centre with the 22nd Infantry Division seizing the abandoned artillery caserne and the Mekenziyevy Mountain train station while the 50th Infantry Division was able to encircle the Forsthaus. However, LIV Corps was less successful in its flank attacks, with the 132nd Infantry Division's attempt to advance its 437th Infantry Regiment towards Fort Maxim Gorky I repulsed twice. Soviet

A Ju 87 Stuka brought down by Soviet fighters or anti-aircraft fire. Fliegerkorps VIII lost three Stukas during Operation *Störfang*, including one shot down by Yak-1 fighters on 29 June. (Central Museum of the Armed Forces, Moscow)

A battery of six 150mm Nebelwerfer 41 multiple rocket launchers firing, with the operator to the left initiating the salvo. Each launcher could fire a salvo of six rockets in ten seconds, to a maximum range of 6,900m. The Eleventh Army had nine batteries of these rocket launchers, which were mainly used to suppress Soviet front-line positions prior to an assault. (Nik Cornish Archive, WH472)

counterattacks from the 95th Rifle Division at 1000hrs and 1300hrs brought the 132nd Infantry Division's advance to a complete halt. On the corps' left flank, the 24th Infantry Division was hung up in the woods near the Eihöhe, repulsing repeated Soviet counterattacks. At 1030hrs on 9 June, the Soviets again committed a company of T-26s from the 81st Tank Battalion to block any further German advance in this area. Meanwhile, Petrov pulled the remnants of the battered 172nd Rifle Division out of the line and moved up the 345th Rifle Division to prevent a breakout from the Mekenziyevy Mountain railway station. 10 June was a relatively quiet day for both sides, with the only significant action occurring around the Forsthaus, where the 50th Infantry Division eliminated the 79th Naval Infantry Brigade's second-echelon units. Hansen also committed the 213th Infantry Regiment to re-energize 132nd Infantry Division's advance along the Haccius Ridge toward Fort Maxim Gorky I. During 9–10 June, LIV Corps suffered another 2,772 casualties.

Petrov realized that the battle was starting to go against him by this point and he ordered the commanders of Defensive Sectors III and IV to mount a pincer attack on the morning of 11 June to cut off the German forces in the area around the Forsthaus. For the first time, the Soviets committed most of their artillery to support the counterattack but it was not enough to counterbalance the German advantage in air support. The counterattacks against the 132nd Infantry Division on Haccius Ridge were repulsed, but the counterattack by the much-reduced 79th Naval Infantry Brigade and the 345th Rifle Division briefly succeeded in penetrating into the boundary between the 50th and 24th Infantry Divisions, (see the battle scene on pages 56–57) with some Soviet infantry getting within 1km of the Forsthaus. However, the attacking Soviet infantry were too depleted to sustain the counterattacks and German ground support aircraft mercilessly strafed and hit them with anti-personnel bombs. Hansen followed up the Soviet counterattack with a push in the centre by the 22nd Infantry Division that advanced to the base of the hill on which Fort Stalin lay and created a bulge in the Soviet line. The next day was relatively quiet, although the Soviets mounted two more small counterattacks against the 213th Infantry Regiment on Haccius Ridge and the 50th Infantry Division pushed the Soviets back from the Forsthaus. Operations on 11–12 June had cost Hansen another 1,957 casualties but the Soviet defences on the north shore were now stretched very thin and virtually all their reserves had been committed to the battle – one more push might finish them. The only question was whether Hansen's tired infantry could break the defenders before their own infantry replacements and ammunition gave out.

On the southern coast, Fretter-Pico ordered the 28th Light Division to make another attempt to secure the high ground on the Vermilion and Rose Hills, but instead became locked in an indecisive battle of attrition with the 381st Rifle Regiment. Between 8 and 10 June, XXX Corps suffered 496 casualties and achieved absolutely nothing against Novikov's 109th Rifle Division. After four days of fruitless limited attacks, Fretter-Pico finally began his main attack on the centre of the Soviet Defensive Sector II in the early morning of 11 June. Müller-Gebhard's 72nd Infantry Division committed its 401st Infantry Regiment to break through the centre of the Soviet line between Chapel Hill and Kamary. After a relatively short artillery preparation, I/401st Infantry Regiment attacked Ruin Hill on the south-west edge of Chapel Hill and succeeded in seizing the position with the help of assault guns. Farther south, III/401st Infantry Regiment succeeded in pushing a salient into the Soviet lines south of the fortified village of Kamary, which was held in strength by the 388th Rifle Division. On 11–12 June the 401st Infantry Regiment continued to attack with all three battalions, supported by part of the 124th Infantry Regiment and gradually began to push in the Soviet defences around Kamary. Polkovnik Nikolai F. Skutel'nik, commander of Defensive Sector II, decided to pull the two weakened battalions of the 778th Rifle Regiment out of Kamary – which was being pounded into rubble by XXX Corps' artillery – and replace them with his reserve battalions. However, the Soviet attempt to conduct a relief in place coincided with a major attack by the 72nd Infantry Division that succeeded in pushing a 2km wedge into the Soviet lines. While the 124th Infantry Regiment pushed through dense minefields to seize Kamary, the 401st Infantry Regiment and 72nd Reconnaissance Group (heavy armoured cars) succeeded in breaking through the 602nd Rifle Regiment's positions on the causeway road. Once the Soviet line became fluid, with some units pulling out of Kamary quickly, Müller-Gebhard committed his divisional reserve – the 266th Infantry Regiment. This regiment quickly marched into the crumbling Soviet forward defences and seized the Soviet artillery positions at Fort Kuppe (which was the site of Redoubt No. 1 in 1854 during the charge of the British Light Brigade). The loss of Kamary was serious, but the Soviets still held important parts of their outer defences in Defensive Sector II and the main defensive belt on Sapun Ridge was intact. Soviet casualties in Defensive Sectors I and II between 7 and 12 June were at least 2,500, including about 700 captured. However, by 13 June XXX Corps had suffered 2,659 casualties, including 394 killed.

An assault group from the German 24th Infantry Division attacks across the southern end of the Kamyschly Ravine on the morning of 7 June 1942. A 115-man spearhead from the 1st Battalion, 32nd Infantry Regiment, had to charge across this stream under fire, penetrate through a minefield and attack up a steep slope into a labyrinth of trenches and bunkers known as 'the block', which was held by a rifle company of the Soviet 2nd Perekop Regiment. Note the use of smoke and hand grenades at the ready. German assault tactics emphasized small, heavily armed teams moving aggressively, rather than large wave attacks. (HITM Photo Research)

FORT STALIN, 13 JUNE

In order to reach the north edge of Severnaya Bay, Hansen's LIV Corps would have to seize Forts Stalin and Volga on top of a large hill south of the train station. The Soviet garrison in Fort Stalin consisted of Captain Nikolai A. Vorobyev's 365th Battery of the 61st Flak Regiment (4 x 76.2mm anti-aircraft guns) and some supporting infantry from the 1st Battalion/1165th Rifle Regiment (345th Rifle Division) – a total of less than 200 troops.[10] The 'fort' was actually a reinforced concrete anti-aircraft position, surrounded by a 4m-thick barbed-wire obstacle. Three concrete machine-gun bunkers provided protection against close assault from the east and south, but Stalin was vulnerable to assault from the north. Both inside and outside the wire obstacle belt, the Soviet defenders had dug deep connecting trenches with overhead cover, enabling them to move around under artillery fire. There were also a number of earth and timber bunkers that protected the approaches to the main position. Fort Stalin was a well-built field fortification and the defenders knew that they were expected to fight to the death.

Generalmajor Wolff chose the relatively fresh 16th Infantry Regiment under Oberst von Choltitz to lead the assault on Fort Stalin. Von Choltitz's regiment had lost five company commanders killed since 7 June, but still had 813 troops fit for combat when the order was received on the afternoon of 12 June to move from their reserve position to an assembly area near the train station. Von Choltitz decided to use I Battalion, with about 200 troops under Major Johannes Arndt, as his main effort. Five StuG III assault guns, an engineer company and a section of *Panzerjäger* with two 37mm guns would follow close behind Arndt's battalion. Hauptmann Hermann-Albert Schrader's III Battalion, with about 110 troops, would support the main effort by clearing the western slope of Stalin. A *Kampfgruppe* comprised of a machine-gun company and the regimental infantry guns would attempt to suppress the Soviet mortars and machine guns known to be located in the Wolf's Ravine on the south-east side of Fort Stalin.

The 306th Army Artillery Command and Fliegerkorps VIII were tasked to suppress Stalin's defenders prior to the attack and to isolate it from receiving any reinforcements. Although 'Dora' had failed to neutralize Stalin, a series of Stuka attacks and 11 420mm mortar rounds on the afternoon of 12 June succeeded in knocking out three of the four 76.2mm gun positions. At 1900hrs, the 22nd Infantry Division's divisional artillery, supplemented by a battery of 210mm mortars and several 280mm and 305mm weapons, began pounding both Stalin and the nearby Fort Volga.

Von Choltitz began moving his regiment towards Fort Stalin at 0300hrs on 13 June but like many night assaults, the friction of combat quickly began to unravel the plan. Arndt's I Battalion attempted to infiltrate in small groups up the north side of the hill but was detected on the slope and began receiving mortar and machine-gun fire from the Wolf's Ravine. The German artillery barrage failed to suppress the Soviet mortar teams located on the reverse slope in the ravine, and they fired salvo after salvo down on the north slope of the hill. This flanking fire caused Arndt to shift his battalion westwards into the supporting III Battalion's sector, resulting in the mixing of both units. Two of the lead company commanders in the I Battalion were also wounded, adding to the confusion. Nevertheless, the remaining German officers and NCOs

---

10. Vorobyev had been awarded the Hero of the Soviet Union for his role in the December 1941 defence.

An MG34 team from the 50th Infantry Division advances at the double, July 1942. German squad offensive and defensive tactics were built around getting the light machine gun into an effective firing position, so the light weight of the MG34 was a distinct advantage. (HITM Photo Research)

took charge and began engaging the outlying infantry fighting positions. By 0400hrs the assault teams had penetrated Stalin's wire obstacle, but all four company commanders were down and the assault slowed as each trench had to be cleared in turn with hand grenades. The five assault guns from Hauptmann Casar's 1st Battery, 190th Assault Gun Battalion, engaged bunkers at point-blank range with 75mm high-explosive rounds. Pioneers from Oberleutnant Heyer's 3rd Company, 744th Pioneer Battalion, also succeeded in flushing out several bunkers with demolition charges and smoke grenades. The three concrete machine-gun bunkers – which faced the wrong way – were finally knocked out when the attached *Panzerjäger* dragged a 37mm Pak 36 gun to within 15m of the back of each one and fired a hollow charge round into it. Some of the Soviet defenders surrendered once their bunkers came under attack, but at least 30 fought to the death inside one bunker while others continued to hold out.

Just as most of the fighting was ebbing on Stalin around 0530hrs, the Soviets began to respond. Fort Volga, located 425m south-west of Stalin, fired mortars and anti-tank guns at the Germans, who were now visible at dawn. Three assault guns were quickly hit and the others obliged to pull back down the hill. Around 0630hrs a Soviet company-sized counterattack was launched out of the Wolf's Ravine but was repulsed by MG34 fire from the support *Kampfgruppe*. Soviet divisional artillery also began to pound Stalin once it became apparent that the position had been lost and this fire killed Hauptmann Schrader.

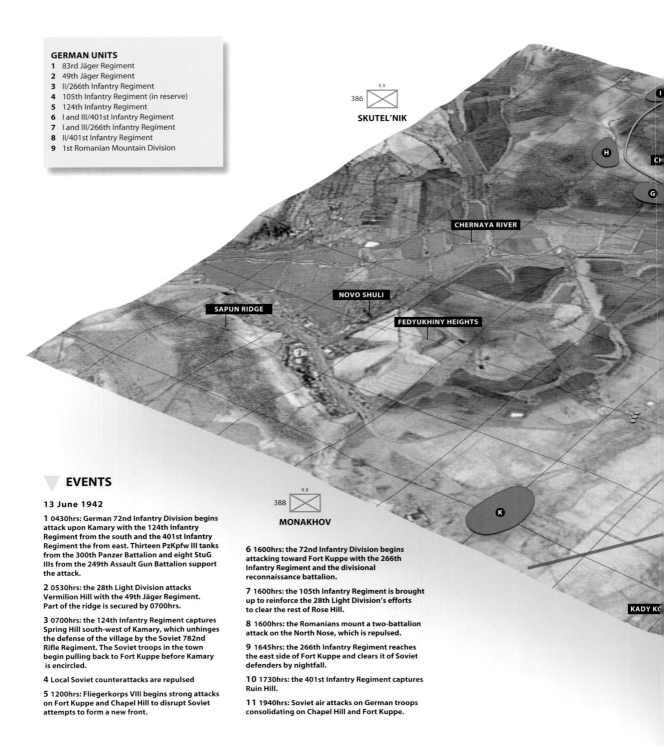

GERMAN UNITS
1 83rd Jäger Regiment
2 49th Jäger Regiment
3 II/266th Infantry Regiment
4 105th Infantry Regiment (in reserve)
5 124th Infantry Regiment
6 I and III/401st Infantry Regiment
7 I and III/266th Infantry Regiment
8 II/401st Infantry Regiment
9 1st Romanian Mountain Division

386 ⊠ ✕✕
SKUTEL'NIK

CHERNAYA RIVER

NOVO SHULI

SAPUN RIDGE

FEDYUKHINY HEIGHTS

H
G
K

▼ **EVENTS**

13 June 1942

1 0430hrs: German 72nd Infantry Division begins attack upon Kamary with the 124th Infantry Regiment from the south and the 401st Infantry Regiment the from east. Thirteen PzKpfw III tanks from the 300th Panzer Battalion and eight StuG IIIs from the 249th Assault Gun Battalion support the attack.

2 0530hrs: the 28th Light Division attacks Vermilion Hill with the 49th Jäger Regiment. Part of the ridge is secured by 0700hrs.

3 0700hrs: the 124th Infantry Regiment captures Spring Hill south-west of Kamary, which unhinges the defense of the village by the Soviet 782nd Rifle Regiment. The Soviet troops in the town begin pulling back to Fort Kuppe before Kamary is encircled.

4 Local Soviet counterattacks are repulsed

5 1200hrs: Fliegerkorps VIII begins strong attacks on Fort Kuppe and Chapel Hill to disrupt Soviet attempts to form a new front.

388 ⊠ ✕✕
MONAKHOV

6 1600hrs: the 72nd Infantry Division begins attacking toward Fort Kuppe with the 266th Infantry Regiment and the divisional reconnaissance battalion.

7 1600hrs: the 105th Infantry Regiment is brought up to reinforce the 28th Light Division's efforts to clear the rest of Rose Hill.

8 1600hrs: the Romanians mount a two-battalion attack on the North Nose, which is repulsed.

9 1645hrs: the 266th Infantry Regiment reaches the east side of Fort Kuppe and clears it of Soviet defenders by nightfall.

10 1730hrs: the 401st Infantry Regiment captures Ruin Hill.

11 1940hrs: Soviet air attacks on German troops consolidating on Chapel Hill and Fort Kuppe.

KADY K

XXX CORPS ATTACK AT CHAPEL HILL, 13 JUNE 1942

After a week of virtually no progress, XXX Corps finally stages a breakthrough attack with the 72nd Infantry Division that punches a salient into the 388th Rifle Division's outer defensive line. However, Soviet resistance in this sector is far from broken and considerable fighting is still be required to secure the vital flank positions on Rose Hill and the North Nose.

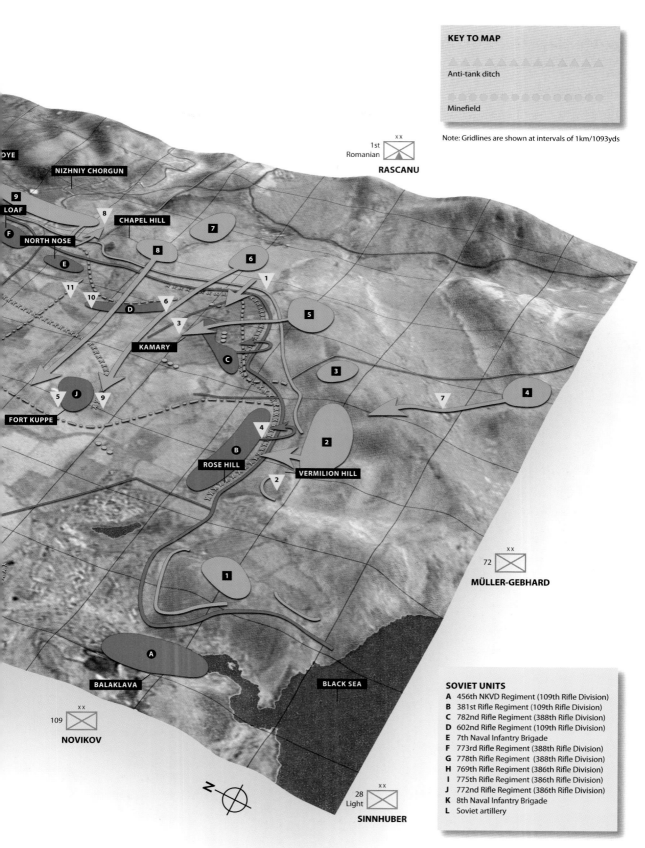

KEY TO MAP

▲▲▲▲▲▲▲▲▲▲▲▲▲ Anti-tank ditch

●●●●●●●●●●●●●●●● Minefield

Note: Gridlines are shown at intervals of 1km/1093yds

OYE

NIZHNIY CHORGUN

9

LOAF

F

NORTH NOSE

E

11

10

D

6

KAMARY

3

C

5

J

9

FORT KUPPE

8

CHAPEL HILL

8

7

6

1

5

3

B

ROSE HILL

4

2

VERMILION HILL

2

7

4

1

A

BALAKLAVA

BLACK SEA

1st
Romanian | X X | ⊠ |
RASCANU

72 | X X | ⊠ |
MÜLLER-GEBHARD

28
Light | X X | ⊠ |
SINNHUBER

109 | X X | ⊠ |
NOVIKOV

SOVIET UNITS
A 456th NKVD Regiment (109th Rifle Division)
B 381st Rifle Regiment (109th Rifle Division)
C 782nd Rifle Regiment (388th Rifle Division)
D 602nd Rifle Regiment (109th Rifle Division)
E 7th Naval Infantry Brigade
F 773rd Rifle Regiment (388th Rifle Division)
G 778th Rifle Regiment (388th Rifle Division)
H 769th Rifle Regiment (386th Rifle Division)
I 775th Rifle Regiment (386th Rifle Division)
J 772nd Rifle Regiment (386th Rifle Division)
K 8th Naval Infantry Brigade
L Soviet artillery

The Germans declared Fort Stalin secured around 0700hrs, although some bunkers held out until 1500hrs. The assault had cost the 16th Infantry Regiment 32 killed, 136 wounded and two missing – about half the infantry committed. Virtually all the German infantry officers involved in the attack were casualties and the regimental adjutant was sent in to organize the defence on Stalin. Most of the Soviet garrison was dead, with only 20 captured. Although I/16th Infantry Regiment had only 91 combat-effective men left on the objective, Petrov made no attempt to recover Fort Stalin, which would prove to be a grave error.

LOSSES MOUNT ON BOTH SIDES, 14–16 JUNE

With Fort Stalin captured and the centre of the Soviet defence in the northern area nearly broken, Hansen decided to switch focus and eliminate the threat to his left flank. While Fort Maxim Gorky I's 305mm guns had played little role in the current battle, the Soviet 95th Rifle Division had been particularly aggressive in counterattacking the flank of the 132nd Infantry Division on Haccius Ridge. Von Manstein was forced to reinforce the 132nd first with the 213th Infantry Regiment and then with two battalions of the 97th Infantry Regiment from the idle 46th Infantry Division at Kerch. One flaw in von Manstein's plan was that only a weak German covering force was left to hold the 3km front from the sea to the town of Belbek, which meant that the 95th Rifle Division in this sector was free to use its reserve battalions for counterattacks.

On 14 June, the 132nd Infantry Division attacked with two battalions of the 437th Infantry Regiment and succeeded in advancing about 300m south of Haccius Ridge. The next day, the 132nd attacked with five battalions and advanced to within 900m of Bastion I. Counterattacks by the 95th Rifle Division continued but were much weaker. On 16 June, the 132nd Infantry Division, now with eight infantry battalions on line, consolidated its hold on the area of the anti-tank ditch west of Haccius Ridge while an ad hoc force of pioneers and *Panzerjäger* began to clear out the Belbek River Valley. During this period of 14–17 June, LIV Corps focused on pulverizing the Soviet forces in Defensive Sector IV, while the 50th Infantry and the 4th Romanian Mountain Divisions slowly pushed the 25th and 345th Rifle Divisions back toward the Martynovski Ravine.

Petrov had few reserves to spare, but two battalions of the 7th Naval Infantry Brigade were sent to reinforce the 345th Rifle Division on 11 June. The 79th Naval Infantry Brigade was still in the line but had been reduced to only 35 per cent strength. By the time that Fort Stalin fell, the 345th Rifle Division's three rifle regiments defending the area between Forts Volga and Siberia were down to about 400 infantry each. The Soviet line was still relatively strong in Defensive Sector III, but Defensive Sector IV was on the verge of collapse. Blocking the way to Fort Maxim Gorky I were three battalions of the 95th Rifle Division and two battalions of the 7th Naval Infantry Brigade, a total of only 1,000 troops.

In the south, Fretter-Pico's offensive continued to expand the dent made in the Soviet lines on 13 June, with the 72nd and 170th Infantry Divisions advancing west another 1,300m on 14–15 June. On 16–17 June, Novikov finally decided to abandon the hotly contested Rose Hill and pulled his forces back toward the town of Kadykovka, north of Balaklava. Slowly, the Soviet outer defences gave way and the 386th and 388th Rifle Divisions were forced back toward the Sapun Ridge. On 18 June, the German 72nd Reconnaissance Battalion under Major Karl Baake slipped through a gap in the Soviet lines and seized a hill known as the Eagle's Perch, which was on the southern approaches to the Sapun Ridge. Between 18 and 20 June, the Romanian 1st Mountain Division was finally able to seize North Nose, Sugar Loaf and the Denkmal Bridge, thereby clearing XXX Corps' right flank. Between 14 and 20 June, XXX Corps had suffered another 2,646 casualties and advanced 3km through the centre of the Soviet outer defences, destroying much of the 388th Rifle Division in the process. XXX Corps had captured about 1,100 prisoners in this period, but few heavy weapons. On 15 June, a battery of four Soviet 82mm mortars were captured along with 1,500 mortar bombs – a clear indication that the forward Soviet units were not running short of ammunition even after two weeks of battle. Furthermore, the Soviets still had a firm grip upon the coast at Balaklava and the Germans had not yet even reached the main defensive belt on Sapun Ridge.

BREAKTHROUGH, 17 JUNE

Around 0500hrs on 17 June, Hansen unleashed a full-scale assault by the reinforced 132nd Infantry Division against the 95th Rifle Division's thin defensive line around Fort Maxim Gorky I, while the 22nd and 24th Infantry Divisions advanced to smash through the centre of the Soviet defences around the train station. Part of the 24th Infantry Division had been brought over from the corps' left flank and inserted between the 132nd and 22nd Infantry Divisions; the infusion of new strength in this area allowed a major thrust toward Fort Molotov and the town of Bartenyevka. The 132nd Infantry Division also conducted a reinforced probe with its reconnaissance battalion on the coast toward the town of Lyubimovka and caught the thinned-out Soviet 161st Rifle Regiment by surprise. A massive artillery and continuous air attack barrage preceded all the attacks, which finally took its toll on Soviet morale. Hit along its entire front simultaneously, the 95th Rifle Division

A German pioneer team attacking a Soviet position with a Flammenwerfer 41 flame-thrower. Each pioneer battalion in LIV Corps had 10–12 flame-throwers, and they were particularly effective at driving Soviet troops out of underground bunkers. The Flammenwerfer 41 weighed 22kg and it had enough fuel for ten seconds of use; it had a maximum range of 30m. (HITM Photo Research)

The fight for Fort Maxim Gorky I, 17–25 June 1942

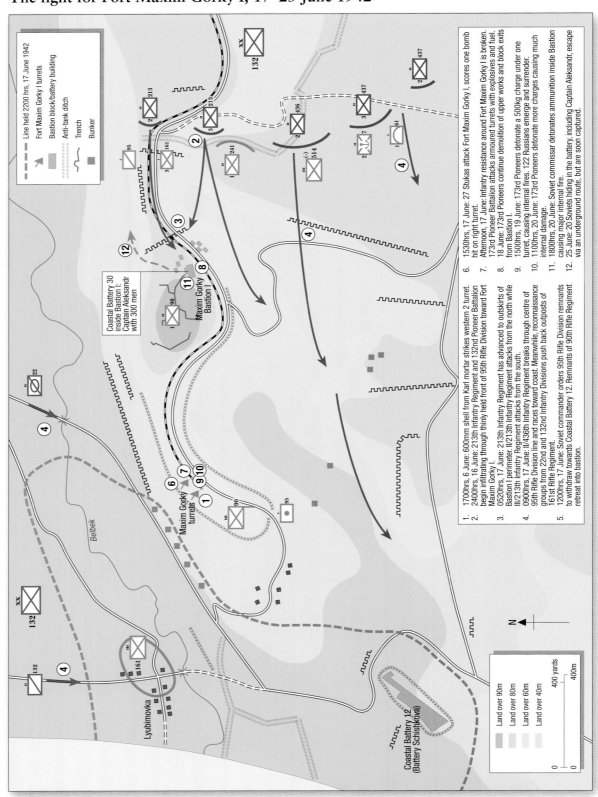

Legend:
- Line held 2200 hrs, 17 June 1942
- Fort Maxim Gorky I turrets
- Bastion block/battery building
- Anti-tank ditch
- Trench
- Bunker

Coastal Battery 30 inside Bastion I: Captain Aleksandr with 300 men

Maxim Gorky Bastion I

Maxim Gorky turrets

Belbek

Lyubimovka

Coastal Battery 12 (Battery Schishkova)

N

- Land over 90m
- Land over 80m
- Land over 60m
- Land over 40m

0   400 yards
0   400m

1. 1700hrs, 6 June: 600mm shell from Karl mortar strikes western 2 turret.
2. 2400hrs, 16 June: 213th Infantry Regiment and 132nd Pioneer Battalion begin infiltrating through thinly held front of 95th Rifle Division toward Fort Maxim Gorky I.
3. 0520hrs, 17 June: 213th Infantry Regiment has advanced to outskirts of Bastion I perimeter. II/213th Infantry Regiment attacks from the north while III/213th Infantry Regiment attacks from the south.
4. 0900hrs, 17 June: II/436th Infantry Regiment breaks through centre of 95th Rifle Division line and races toward coast. Meanwhile, reconnaissance groups from 22nd and 132nd Infantry Divisions push back outposts of 161st Rifle Regiment.
5. 1200hrs, 17 June: Soviet commander orders 95th Rifle Division remnants to withdraw towards Coastal Battery 12. Remnants of 90th Rifle Regiment retreat into bastion.
6. 1530hrs, 17 June: 27 Stukas attack Fort Maxim Gorky I, scores one bomb hit on right turret.
7. Afternoon, 17 June: Infantry resistance around Fort Maxim Gorky I is broken. 173rd Pioneer Battalion attacks armoured turrets with explosives and fuel.
8. 18 June: 173rd Pioneers continue demolition of upper works and block exits from Bastion I.
9. 1500hrs, 19 June: 173rd Pioneers detonate a 500kg charge under one turret, causing internal fires. 122 Russians emerge and surrender.
10. 1100hrs, 20 June: 173rd Pioneers detonate more charges causing much internal damage.
11. 1800hrs, 20 June: Soviet commissar detonates ammunition inside Bastion causing major internal fire.
12. 25 June: 20 Soviets hiding in the battery, including Captain Aleksandr, escape via an underground route, but are soon captured.

68

collapsed and by 0520hrs German infantry had achieved a breakthrough south of Fort Maxim Gorky I. The survivors of the 95th Rifle Division fell back along the coast to form a perimeter around Lyubimovka and Coastal Battery 12 – Fort Maxim Gorky I was left to its fate.

German infantry from the 436th and 437th Infantry Regiments were already behind Fort Maxim Gorky I by 0900hrs but it was not until the afternoon that the 132nd Infantry Division devoted any real effort to dealing with the fort. An attack by 27 Stukas at 1630hrs scored a direct hit on the western turret and the guns were now out of ammunition and silent. About 300 Soviet naval gunners and infantry stragglers from the 95th Rifle Division were holding out in Bastion I and the turret block, which were connected by an underground 600m-long tunnel. The 173rd Pioneer Battalion was assigned to

A German pioneer cuts through the Soviet barbed wire under cover of smoke shells. German assault troops had to quickly break through the obstacle belt of wire and mines before the Soviets caught them in their 'kill zone'. (Anne S. K. Brown)

dig out the garrison and it proceeded to demolish the turrets, but it could not gain access to the interior of the fort. Now began a three-day effort to reduce the fort, which was not resolved until 20 June.

Meanwhile in the centre, the 22nd and 24th Infantry Divisions had actually begun to move assault groups forward around 0330hrs and quickly penetrated the weak Soviet line around the train station. The 31st Infantry Regiment attacked a Soviet outpost on a hill position known as the Annaberg that blocked the Harbour Road down to Severnaya Bay. For the first time, the Germans used six B IV remote-control demolition vehicles against the trenches and bunkers on the Annaberg, but with unimpressive results. One B IV exploded prematurely, killing its handlers, and two others were disabled in a minefield. Two PzKpfw III control tanks were also destroyed by Soviet anti-tank fire. Only two of six B IVs actually reached the Soviet trenches, destroying a couple of timber bunkers. Despite this inauspicious start, the two infantry battalions of the 31st Infantry Regiment soon took the Annaberg and pressed on to take Fort Siberia by surprise, capturing it by 0510hrs. Once dawn broke, the 306th Army Artillery Command massed three *Nebelwerfer* battalions from the 1st Heavy Mortar Regiment to provide the preparation barrage for the 24th Infantry Division and the multiple rocket launchers did great damage to the Soviet forward infantry positions. Von Tettau attacked with the 31st and 102nd Infantry Regiments, supported by two assault gun batteries with 19 StuG IIIs and two Panzer companies from the 300th Panzer Battalion with PzKpfw III tanks. The 24th Infantry Division's attack achieved rapid success and overran Fort Tscheka, Fort GPU at 0700hrs, then Fort Molotov at 0745hrs, and soon reached the outskirts of Bartenyevka. On von Tettau's left flank, the 22nd Infantry Division used its position on Fort Stalin and Fort Siberia to put pressure on the Soviet defences in this area and succeeded in capturing Fort Volga by 1930hrs. Von Richthofen's Fliegerkorps

VIII committed all its operational aircraft to a series of concentrated attacks upon the North Bay area starting at 1120hrs and by noon Petrov no longer had a coherent defence on the north side of Severnaya Bay.

The attack had gained up to 2km in the centre and had isolated or destroyed the bulk of Soviet units in Defensive Sectors III and IV; the 95th and 172nd Rifle Divisions. Only the 25th Rifle Division was still in the line and combat effective by the end of 17 June. Petrov rushed up the 138th Naval Infantry Brigade, which had landed on 12–13 June, to strengthen the defence. The appearance of this fresh unit with over 2,600 troops prevented the Germans from reaching Severnaya Bay that day. Nevertheless, Hansen's LIV Corps had accomplished its objectives, albeit at the cost of another 1,000 casualties.

COLLAPSE OF DEFENSIVE SECTOR IV, 18–23 JUNE

Most of what remained of the 95th Rifle Division and their support troops were huddled in a 2km-long pocket wedged against the Black Sea coast, from the town of Lyubimovka to Coastal Battery 12 (known as Battery Schishkova to the Germans). The 132nd Infantry Division wasted no time moving against these survivors and the 436th Infantry Regiment launched a deliberate assault against Coastal Battery 12 at 1100hrs on 18 June. Oberleutnant Wack's 2nd Company, 3rd Pioneer Battalion, led the assault and was able to gain entry into the northern part of the battery by 1900hrs. Plentifully supplied with demolition charges and flame-throwers, Wack's men methodically cleared out the casemates while the supporting infantry suppressed trenches on both sides of the battery. The last defenders were not rooted out until 0900hrs on 19 June when 36 naval gunners finally surrendered. Wack's pioneers had suffered seven killed, 14 wounded and one missing in the fight for the battery. Once Coastal Battery 12 surrendered, the remaining survivors of the 95th Rifle Division soon gave up.

Meanwhile, the rest of Hansen's LIV Corps pushed hard against the tottering Soviet defensive lines north of Severnaya Bay. Bartenyevka fell to the 24th Infantry Division on 18 June while the 22nd Infantry Division advanced to the edge of the Wolf's Ravine. However, the Soviets on the north side of Severnaya Bay still had some fight left and Petrov ordered the 138th Naval Infantry Brigade to conduct a battalion-sized counterattack into the left flank

A casualty arrives at a German field hospital, in a Phänomen Granit 25H ambulance (Kfz 31). An infantry division usually had two ambulance platoons, each with eight ambulances. (Nik Cornish Archive, WH388)

A German minesweeping team uses probes to search for Soviet mines on a dirt road. The Soviet defenders at Sevastopol used both TMD 40 anti-tank mines and PMD-6 anti-personnel mines. Each corps was clearing over 1,000 mines per day and was forced to use Tatar 'volunteers' and some Soviet POWs for mine clearance. (Nik Cornish Archive, WH544)

of the 22nd Infantry Division at 0400hrs on 19 June. The 138th Naval Infantry Brigade and remnants of the 79th Naval Infantry Brigade held a fortified hill at the end of the bay that the Germans had dubbed the Jewish Nose.[11] This hilltop, overlooking the old harbour, was the last major defensible position that the Soviets held on the north-east side of the bay. The Soviet counterattack failed because of lack of artillery or air support. By 20 June, the 22nd Infantry Division had advanced to within sight of Severnaya Bay.

The 24th Infantry Division attacked Battery Lenin and the adjoining North Fort at 0900hrs on 20 June. Battery Lenin was held by the 366th Anti-Aircraft Battery, which had already lost three of its four 76mm anti-aircraft guns to artillery bombardment. Apparently the morale of this unit had been broken by days of bombardment and when the German I/97th Infantry Regiment and 132nd Pioneer Battalion attacked Battery Lenin, the 80-man garrison surrendered post-haste. However, the North Fort was a 300m-long 19th-century concrete star-shaped, fort protected by a 5m-wide anti-tank ditch and over 1,000 mines. Inside the North Fort, there were 32 concrete bunkers, seven armoured cupolas and 70 earth-and-timber bunkers, making it a formidable position. The command post of the 61st Anti-Aircraft Regiment was located in a casemate inside the North Fort. The assault troops from the II/31st Infantry Regiment and the 24th Pioneer Battalion approached from the east side of the North Fort by using a bombed-out naval infantry barracks block for cover, but when they crossed the intervening open space they were met by a hail of machine-gun fire. The 300th Panzer Battalion brought up three of its B IV radio-controlled demolition vehicles, but as soon as the slow-moving vehicles left cover they were shot to pieces in a hail of anti-tank fire. It took nine hours of fighting for the pioneers and infantrymen just to break into the outer works of the North Fort, and the exhausted assault group broke off the attack at nightfall. The German assault troops renewed the attack on the morning of 21 June and soon broke into the centre of the North Fort. By 1130hrs the fort was in German hands, along with 182 prisoners.

11. The fact that such a racist epithet was used as the name of an operational objective on Eleventh Army maps is further evidence of von Manstein's adoption of Nazi views on race.

GERMAN ASSAULT PIONEERS DEMOLISH COASTAL BATTERY 30 (FORT MAXIM GORKY I), 18 JUNE 1942

In the spring of 1914, the Russian Navy began preparation of a site for a new coastal battery on a ridgeline on the south side of the Belbek River, but World War I interrupted the work. After the end of that war and the subsequent Russian Civil War, the new Communist regime decided to complete the project. Coastal Battery 30 was completed in 1933 and consisted of two twin 305mm gun turrets mounted atop a buried concrete casemate that was connected by a tunnel to a reinforced battery control centre (later dubbed 'Bastion I' by the Germans).

During the siege of Sevastopol, Coastal Battery 30, under the command of Captain Georg Aleksandr, fired 1,238 305mm shells during the fighting in November–December 1941. By the spring of 1942, the gun barrels were worn out and ammunition was scarce, so the battery fired very sparingly in the final months of the siege. Much of the German bombardment that began on 2 June focused on this battery and on 6 June Turret No. 2 was knocked out by a 600mm concrete-piercing shell from one of the Karl mortars. The battery was hit by eight 800mm rounds from 'Dora', as well as numerous 305mm and 240mm rounds and multiple heavy bombs dropped by Stukas. Although the battery was badly damaged, only 40 of its 300-man garrison were killed or wounded by the bombardment. By 17 June, German infantry from Oberst Otto Hitzfeld's 213th Infantry Regiment had seized the area around the battery, trapping 89 men from the battery and about 130 stragglers from other units in the underground casemates. Hitzfeld called upon the pioneers from the 1st Company, 173rd Pioneer Battalion, to demolish the battery and smoke out the trapped Soviet troops.

This scene depicts the German engineers of the 1st Company, 173rd Pioneer Battalion, attempting to burn out the trapped Soviet garrison from the two gun turrets on the afternoon of 18 June. The area around the turrets is scarred by multiple large shell craters from the German bombardment, including craters from 'Dora' and the Karl mortars (1). Small teams of pioneers move forward using the craters and one team is atop Turret No. 1, attaching two large fuel drums and numerous 30kg satchel charges (2). Meanwhile, a second team is running for cover (3) as the roof of Turret No. 2 explodes in a sheet of flames (4). The pioneers poured gasoline and flammol into the resulting cracks in the 200mm-thick turret roofs and ignited it with flare pistols. Although the explosions caused some internal fires, the Soviet garrison remained inside and the German pioneers could not force their way into the battery. It was not until 1500hrs on 19 June that some 115 Soviets emerged from one of the exits and surrendered, but Captain Aleksandr remained inside with about 100 others. The German pioneers spent another three days attempting to demolish Coastal Battery 30, finally destroying the turrets with 500kg charges. Most of the remaining Soviet garrison surrendered, but Captain Aleksandr and five gunners hid in the underground casemate for several more days and then escaped using an underground draining duct on 24 June. Aleksandr was captured on the morning of 26 June.

Once the North Fort had fallen, Petrov ordered the evacuation of the remaining Soviet troops from the north side of Severnaya Bay, but there were few small boats available and German artillery destroyed those that attempted to make the trip. Instead, most Soviet troops from Defensive Sector IV huddled in the tunnels and caves along the edge of the bay near White Cliff, with their ammunition virtually expended. The 22nd and 24th Infantry Divisions mopped up most of these survivors on 22–23 June. About 800 Soviet wounded waited in buildings near Fort Konstantinovsky, at the north entrance to Severnaya Bay. Fort Konstantinovsky was another relic of the late 19th century and it had been badly damaged by repeated Stuka attacks early in the siege. A group of 74 Soviet naval infantrymen under Captain Yevseyev conducted a last stand in Fort Konstantinovsky until their ammunition was exhausted; 26 were captured by the 24th Infantry Division when the fort fell on the morning of 23 June.

The remnants of Defensive Sector III held a tenuous 4km-long line on the wooded hilltops north of the Martynovski Ravine. Although the 138th Naval Infantry Brigade and the remnants of 2nd Perekop Regiment had a firm defence around the Jewish Nose hill on the east end of the bay, the right flank held by the 25th Rifle Division was virtually dangling in the air, with no good defensive positions. Having finished off Defensive Sector IV, Hansen now moved to put paid to Defensive Sector III. German infantry losses were now severe, with the fighting strength of the three battalions in the 65th Infantry Regiment reduced to about 125 men each, while the 50th Infantry Division's regiments were reduced to about 600 men each. However, the Germans gained an intelligence windfall when two platoon leaders from the 138th Naval Infantry Brigade deserted on 21 June and told the Germans the complete layout of Soviet defences in the area. At 0530hrs on 22 June, the 22nd and 50th Infantry Divisions, as well as a *Kampfgruppe* built around the 132nd Infantry Division's reconnaissance battalion, the 190th Assault Gun Battalion and part of the 72nd Infantry Regiment, 46th Infantry Division, attacked and slowly began pushing the Soviet line back. The Germans employed their favourite tactic, identifying the thinly held boundary between the 25th Rifle Division's 54th and 287th Rifle Regiments, pounding the boundary area with

Soviet naval infantry counterattacking across rocky ground. Note the mix of weapons: the sailor in the foreground is armed with an SVT-40 semi-automatic rifle, the one behind him has a DP light machine gun, while others have Mosin-Nagant bolt action rifles and PPSch-41 sub-machine guns. The Soviets tended to attack in larger groups, often resulting in heavier casualties. (Author's collection)

German assault infantry from the 16th Infantry Regiment moving up the slope toward Fort Stalin on the morning of 13 June. Note that the troops are weighed down with extra machine-gun ammunition boxes and that several have fixed bayonets. (Anne S. K. Brown)

massed artillery, and then pushing an infantry/assault gun *Kampfgruppe* through the gap. The *Kampfgruppe* succeeded in penetrating 2km by the next morning, overrunning part of the 25th Rifle Division and seriously denting the Soviet line. Meanwhile, the 50th Infantry Division attacked and seized the Jewish Nose from the 138th Naval Infantry Brigade, while German pioneers cleared the tunnels out with flame-throwers. By the end of 23 June, Defensive Sector III was falling apart, with the remnants of the 345th Rifle Division trapped in the Wolf's Ravine and the 25th Rifle Division and 79th Naval Infantry Brigade reduced to a total of about four battalions.

XXX CORPS GRINDS FORWARD SLOWLY, 21–28 JUNE 1942

During the fourth week of June, Fretter-Pico's advance finally approached the main Soviet defensive belt on Sapun Ridge. In order to improve his attack frontage prior to assaulting the main Soviet position, Fretter-Pico shifted his axis of advance from due west toward the north and the Fedyukhiny Heights. Polkovnik Skutel'nik, commander of the 386th Rifle Division and Defensive Sector II, had expected a direct assault on the Sapun Ridge and left only his depleted 772nd Rifle Regiment on the Fedyukhiny Heights. During the night of 20/21 June the Germans brought in two battalions of the 420th Infantry Regiment from outside the Eleventh Army to reinforce Sander's 170th Infantry Division. On 21 June Sander attacked the 772nd Rifle Regiment with both the 391st and 420th Infantry Regiments, overrunning most of the Fedyukhiny Heights before Skutel'nik could react. The Romanian 1st Mountain Division, operating on the right flank also advanced about 2km and cleared up the lower Chernaya River Valley and seized a crossing site on the night of 22 June.

Fretter-Pico now had most of the 170th Infantry Division within 1–2km of Sapun Ridge, but his attack ran out of steam. After the successful advance on 21–22 June, XXX Corps virtually shifted to the defence for the next five days, content merely to mop up the small remaining portions of the Fedyukhiny Heights and to enlarge the salient around the Eagle's Perch. Fretter-Pico used this period to reorganize and rest his forces for the final attack on Sapun Ridge. Most of the 28th Light Division was pulled back into reserve, substituting an ad hoc Kriegsmarine naval infantry battalion and a construction battalion to hold the coast near Balaklava. However, Soviet artillery observers atop the

A Soviet rifle battalion moves up through one of the ravines. At Sevastopol, the Soviets placed most of their reserves, artillery and supply depots in such ravines, in order to conceal them from German observation. (Central Museum of the Armed Forces, Moscow)

Sapun Ridge were able to observe much of the German tactical movements below and were still capable of delivering devastating counterbattery barrages.[12] Ten of XXX Corps' artillery pieces were destroyed during 21–28 June, including five 150mm s.FH 18 medium howitzers.

While XXX Corps was temporarily *hors de combat*, the Romanian Mountain Corps took up the slack by launching its first multi-division attack on 24 June. The Romanian 18th Infantry Division, which had not yet been tasked with any major offensive tasks, was ordered to attack towards a heavily fortified Soviet position known as Bastion II on the hills east of the Chernaya River. Supported by about 100 guns from their corps and divisional artillery, all three infantry regiments attacked up the steep, wooded slope but made little progress until joined by the 1st Mountain Division. Finally, Bastion II was seized at 1230hrs on 25 June and the Romanian infantry succeeded in fending off a Soviet counterattack. General-maior Avramescu followed up the success of his corps' attack by ordering the 18th Infantry Division and the newly arrived 4th Mountain Division to continue clearing the ridgeline up to the Chernaya River. By 27 June, the 4th Mountain Division captured the west end of the ridgeline, known as Kegel. On 28 June, the German 132nd Infantry Division from LIV Corps attacked the remnants of Defensive Sector III on Lighthouse Hill and in some of the tunnels on the east end of the bay, eliminating much of the cornered Soviet infantry. Petrov was able to save some of the artillery and withdraw it to the cliffs around Inkerman, but his ammunition was running low.

Hansen's corps linked up with the Romanians and the Axis now held all of the heights east of the Chernaya River.

With LIV Corps and the Romanians poised to assault Sevastopol's final defensive line, Fretter-Pico's corps was ready to rejoin the battle. He massed the bulk of the 170th Infantry Division and the Romanian 1st Mountain Division on the Fedyukhiny Heights, with the 28th Light Division in reserve. Meanwhile the 72nd Infantry Division, stripped of the 105th Infantry Regiment, held the 6km-long front from the Eagle's Perch to Balaklava.

12. These observers were near the spot where Lord Raglan observed the 'charge of the Light Brigade' in 1854.

THE DECISIVE DAY, 29 JUNE 1942

As the end of June approached, von Manstein became increasingly desperate to reduce Sevastopol's final defensive positions before he lost his precious air support. Von Richthofen and his staff had departed for Kharkov on 23 June to prepare for the upcoming *Fall Blau* summer offensive and this presaged the departure of the actual combat squadrons. Luftwaffe sorties in support of Eleventh Army dropped off by a third after von Richthofen left and it was obvious that three weeks of constant combat sorties had drained the crews and depleted the reserves of fuel and bombs. Realizing that the siege was rapidly approaching a culminating point, where the attackers might not have the means to overwhelm the defenders, von Manstein decided to gamble.

Due to the evacuation of the last Soviet troops from the northern shore of Severnaya Bay and the gradual advance of the German XXX Corps in the south, the main Soviet defences now rested upon the cliffs of Inkerman along the Chernaya River Valley and the Sapun Ridge. Petrov placed his best units, the 138th Naval Infantry Brigade and about 250 sailors of the 3rd Naval Infantry Regiment, to hold the critical east end of Severnaya Bay and the bridge over the Chernaya near Inkerman. However, the 138th Naval Infantry Brigade had already suffered about 80 per cent losses in its front-line rifle companies since it was committed on 17 June. The 386th Rifle Division, reinforced by the 7th, 8th and 9th Naval Infantry Brigades, held Sapun Ridge. Petrov still had plentiful artillery and mortars to support his main defensive positions but like von Manstein, he was running out of infantry reserves. To hold the area around Inkerman and the Chernaya River Valley, Petrov had the remnants of the 25th and 345th Rifle Divisions – each equivalent to a weak regiment – along with five construction battalions. Apparently, Petrov was not overly concerned about the defences along Severnaya Bay, leaving this area guarded by the burnt-out 79th Naval Infantry Brigade and the 2nd Perekop Regiment. Although Petrov's situation was desperate, he knew that help in the form of additional reinforcements would soon be forthcoming, unlike von Manstein who could not expect any further reinforcements. Petrov played for time and ordered his depleted infantry to hold in place. Communist commissars ensured that the troops would not retreat, even as they began contemplating their own escapes.

Once fighting ended north of Severnaya Bay, the German 22nd and 24th Infantry Divisions were placed in reserve and the rest of the 132nd Infantry Division was brought around to assist the 50th Infantry Division's advance upon Inkerman. However, a ground assault across the open Chernaya River Valley and the nearby basin area would be very costly, beginning another drawn-out attrition battle that the Eleventh Army could ill afford. Whenever presented with enemy strength, von Manstein looked to envelopment and in this case he decided upon an assault crossing across Severnaya Bay to unhinge the Soviet line at Inkerman. Although this tactic had worked well during Operation *Störfang*, the

An *Unteroffizier* (NCO) from the 24th Infantry Division receives instructions for some of the final attacks at Sevastopol, July 1942. By the end of the battle, German infantry platoons were usually being led by sergeants and excessive small unit leader casualties began to sap the combat effectiveness of the attacking divisions. (HITM Photo Research)

German assault troops from the 1st Company, 173rd Pioneer Battalion, attempting to demolish Turret No. 2 of Fort Maxim Gorky I on 18 June 1942. Although the fort's two turrets were already inoperative, the German pioneers made repeated attempts with explosive charges and improvised fire bombs to get at the gun crews still holding out below ground. (HITM Photo Research)

commanders of the 22nd and 24th Infantry Divisions were less sanguine about getting across the 600m of Severnaya Bay without being shot to pieces by Soviet artillery and machine guns. Nevertheless, von Manstein ordered Hansen to conduct an assault crossing across the bay early on the morning of 29 June with parts of both divisions, while the rest of LIV Corps attacked the Soviet defences around Inkerman. Von Manstein also ordered Fretter-Pico to conduct a night attack upon Sapun Ridge to penetrate the Soviet line in the south. Von Manstein believed that a nearly simultaneous concentric attack would strain the depleted Soviet defences and achieve a breakthrough in one or more locations.

Petrov and Oktyabrsky were aware that the German Eleventh Army had two assault boat units, but they misinterpreted where they might be used. As part of a deception, Italian MAS boats staged a feint landing near Cape Fiolent on the south coast on the night of 27/28 June that apparently convinced Petrov and Oktyabrsky that von Manstein would attempt to land troops behind Defensive Sector I.

After midnight on 28 June, German pioneers began to lay a smokescreen on the north side of Severnaya Bay while the Luftwaffe staged several noisy bomber raids on Sevastopol's dock areas. Meanwhile, assault groups from the 65th Infantry Regiment under Oberst Schitting and 16th Infantry Regiment under Oberst von Choltitz assembled in the Wolf's Ravine and moved to the water's edge. Von Manstein had quietly brought forward the 902nd and 905th Assault Boat Commands, with a total of 130 assault boats. At 0100hrs, about 380 assault troops from the 65th Infantry Regiment embarked in the flimsy craft and began moving across the bay. Hansen decided not to fire an artillery preparation upon the landing area, hoping to achieve maximum surprise. At 0120hrs, the first German assault troops landed just east of the electrical power plant and immediately moved to seize the high ground. The few troops from the 79th Naval Infantry Brigade in the area were caught completely by surprise and were eliminated before they could raise the alarm. At 0145hrs, the first wave of the 16th Infantry Regiment began landing just west of the electrical plant. It was not until 0200hrs that the Soviets awoke to the landing and began firing off red flares to alert brigade headquarters. Although the Soviets were able to block the rapid expansion of the beachhead with several

▼ EVENTS

29 June 1942

1 0200hrs: German engineers lay smokescreen across Severnaya Bay, while 22nd and 24th Infantry Divisions' artillery bombards Soviet trenches on south side of bay.

2 0220hrs: first wave of 65th Infantry Regiment under Schitting crosses Severnaya Bay on 76 assault boats and lands just east of the electrical plant. The 79th Naval Infantry Brigade does not detect the crossing until German infantry disembark.

3 0230hrs: XXX Corps artillery begins preparatory fire on Sapun Ridge.

4 0245hrs: First wave of 16th Infantry Regiment crosses Severnaya Bay on 54 assault boats.

5 0305–0355hrs: 16th and 65th Infantry Regiments seize the heights above the electrical plant, securing the beachhead.

6 0330hrs: 170th Division attacks 7th Naval Infantry Brigade on Sapun Ridge with three reinforced battalions and is atop the ridge by 0340hrs. After four hours of tough fighting in the trench systems, the German assault groups achieve a breakthrough by 0715hrs.

7 0330hrs: Romanian 1st Mountain Division attacks Soviet 775th Rifle Regiment forward positions in village of Novo Shuli with a regimental-sized group. After three hours of house-to-house fighting, the Romanians clear the village.

8 0400hrs: 121st Infantry Regiment attacks main Soviet defensive position near Chernaya River bridge.

9 0450hrs: Fliegerkorps VIII begins rolling Stuka attacks that disrupt Soviet reserves and artillery behind Sapun Ridge.

10 0507hrs: XXX Corps commits its reserve, the 105th Infantry Regiment, to exploit the breakthrough on Sapun Ridge.

11 0605hrs: the 132nd Infantry Division attacks across the Chernaya River valley to seize the south side of Inkerman. Soviet defenses here are weak and despite heavy Soviet mortar fire, the German assault troops soon cross the river and adjacent aqueduct. By nightfall, this unit has taken 1,250 prisoners around Inkerman

12 0700hrs: III/123rd Infantry Regiment seizes Old Fort.

13 1210hrs: Kampfgruppe Walter from the 50th Division attacks westwards to link up with beachhead and cut off Soviet defenders around Inkerman.

14 Afternoon: German engineers get an 8-ton ferry into operation and move a company of *Panzerjäger* and light flak to reinforce the beachhead, as well as the 213th and 47th Infantry Regiments. The 50th Infantry Division is able to link up with the bridgehead, trapping thousands of Soviet troops near Inkerman.

15 By nightfall: XXX Corps has completely cleared Sapun Ridge of Soviet troops and the 28th Light Division's 49th Jäger Regiment has been brought up from reserve to pursue the retreating 386th Rifle Division remnants. By 2100hrs, the 49th Jäger Regiment is near the Soviet artillery positions in the English Cemetery.

MARTINOVSKY RAVINE

JEWISH NOSE HILL

LIGHTHOUSE HILL

GRAYTAN

WOLF'S RAVINE

CHAMPAGNE FACTORY

POLDER

WHITE CLIFFS

INKERMAN

OLD FORT

DOCK

SEVERNAYA BAY

ELECTRICAL PLANT

KILEN BAY

MALAKHOV HILL

KORABELNAYA

ENGLISH CEMETERY

386 X X

SKUTEL'NIK

XXX AND LIV CORPS BREACH SEVASTOPOL'S INNER DEFENSIVE LINE, 29 JUNE 1942

Hansen's LIV Corps stages a surprise assault crossing of Severnaya Bay with the 22nd and 24th Infantry Divisions, while the 50th and 132nd Infantry Divisions cross the Chernaya River and trap the Soviet defenders around Inkerman. Simultaneously, Fretter-Pico's XXX Corps launches its decisive attack upon the Sapun Ridge and achieves a breakthrough.

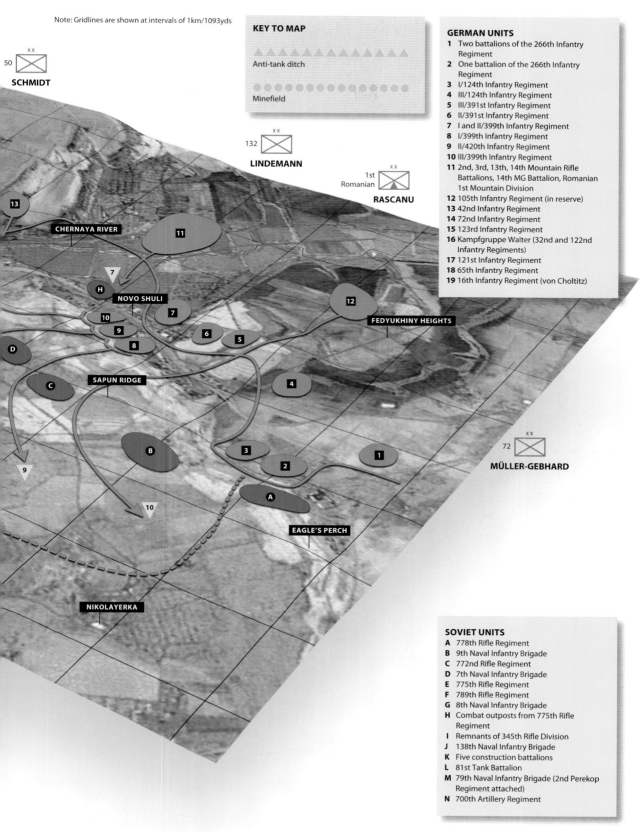

Note: Gridlines are shown at intervals of 1km/1093yds

KEY TO MAP

▲▲▲▲▲▲▲▲▲▲▲▲▲
Anti-tank ditch

●●●●●●●●●●●●●●●
Minefield

xx
50 ⊠
SCHMIDT

xx
132 ⊠
LINDEMANN

xx
1st ⊠
Romanian
RASCANU

xx
72 ⊠
MÜLLER-GEBHARD

CHERNAYA RIVER

NOVO SHULI

FEDYUKHINY HEIGHTS

SAPUN RIDGE

EAGLE'S PERCH

NIKOLAYERKA

GERMAN UNITS

1 Two battalions of the 266th Infantry Regiment
2 One battalion of the 266th Infantry Regiment
3 I/124th Infantry Regiment
4 III/124th Infantry Regiment
5 III/391st Infantry Regiment
6 II/391st Infantry Regiment
7 I and II/399th Infantry Regiment
8 I/399th Infantry Regiment
9 II/420th Infantry Regiment
10 III/399th Infantry Regiment
11 2nd, 3rd, 13th, 14th Mountain Rifle Battalions, 14th MG Battalion, Romanian 1st Mountain Division
12 105th Infantry Regiment (in reserve)
13 42nd Infantry Regiment
14 72nd Infantry Regiment
15 123rd Infantry Regiment
16 Kampfgruppe Walter (32nd and 122nd Infantry Regiments)
17 121st Infantry Regiment
18 65th Infantry Regiment
19 16th Infantry Regiment (von Choltitz)

SOVIET UNITS

A 778th Rifle Regiment
B 9th Naval Infantry Brigade
C 772nd Rifle Regiment
D 7th Naval Infantry Brigade
E 775th Rifle Regiment
F 789th Rifle Regiment
G 8th Naval Infantry Brigade
H Combat outposts from 775th Rifle Regiment
I Remnants of 345th Rifle Division
J 138th Naval Infantry Brigade
K Five construction battalions
L 81st Tank Battalion
M 79th Naval Infantry Brigade (2nd Perekop Regiment attached)
N 700th Artillery Regiment

Aerial view of Coastal Battery 30 after the fighting. The roof of Turret No. 2 has been blown off. Note the large craters from multiple super-heavy artillery rounds. (Ted Nevill, TRH Pictures)

strong platoon-sized positions, they lacked the reserves in this area to launch a serious counterattack. The 81st Tank Battalion, with about six T-26 tanks remaining, was located in a nearby ravine, but Petrov was reluctant to commit it in the dark without proper infantry support. Furthermore, when the Soviet command first learned of the landings, they made the mistaken assumption that it was an airborne assault – which led to great confusion. The quick loss of the high ground overlooking the landing sites meant that the Soviets could not observe the crossings. Instead, the Soviets were content to sporadically shell the suspected landing sites with their organic mortars and wait for daylight to figure out what was happening on the bay. Although Soviet artillery fire succeeded in damaging nearly a quarter of the assault boats by sunrise, only two boats were destroyed and the German pioneers suffered only four killed and 29 wounded.

Petrov's delay in counterattacking the landing was fatal for the defence of Sevastopol. Off to the south, XXX Corps began its artillery preparation on Sapun Ridge at 0130hrs, with the main weight falling on the 7th Naval Infantry Brigade and the 775th Rifle Regiment in the centre of the ridgeline. Prisoner interrogations had revealed the location of the 386th Rifle Division's command post behind the ridge and the German artillerymen succeeded in hitting it, wounding both the commander Polkovnik Skutel'nik and his commissar. Meanwhile, German multi-barrelled *Nebelwerfer* laid a heavy barrage of high explosive and smoke upon the top of the ridge. Fretter-Pico assigned Sander's 170th Infantry Division the mission of conducting the night assault and he moved up three relatively fresh battalions into assault positions just below the ridge on the evening of 28 June. The three assault battalions were reinforced with a battery of assault guns, a company of PzKpfw III Ausf. J tanks from the 300th Panzer Battalion and a flak battery. At 0230hrs the assault troops advanced upon the ridge, suffering significant losses from the surviving Soviet mortars and machine guns. However, the assault troops were atop the ridge in strength by 0340hrs and became involved in a vicious close-quarter fight in the dark in the trenches with the 4th Battalion of the 7th Naval Infantry Brigade. The Soviet naval infantrymen fought desperately to hold their positions, but they fought alone. Under conditions of limited visibility, the 300th Panzer Battalion was able to conduct several successful remote-control attacks against Soviet bunkers and one 76mm gun position was destroyed. In order to support XXX Corps' attack, the Romanian 1st Mountain Division launched a regimental-sized attack on the village of Novo-Shuli and captured it after three hours of house-to-house fighting.

At morning twilight, Fliegerkorps VIII's Stukas began rolling attacks near the Serpentine on the ridge in order to further disrupt the 386th Rifle Division. Once Fretter-Pico realized that the 170th Infantry Division was achieving success in the centre of the ridgeline, he committed his reserve – the 105th Infantry Regiment – to widen the breach. The fresh German unit followed behind the four reserve battalions of the 391st and 399th Infantry Regiments that were now joining the assault echelon atop the ridge; however instead of joining the close battle, the 105th Infantry Regiment pivoted to the south-west and enveloped the Soviet 9th Naval Infantry Brigade near the Serpentine. Lacking reserves or effective command and control, the units of the 386th Rifle Division were gradually isolated and overwhelmed. By 0715hrs, XXX Corps had achieved a breakthrough on Sapun Ridge, although Soviet resistance would not be broken until the afternoon.

Captain Georg Aleksandr, commander of Coastal Battery 30 (known to the Germans as Fort Maxim Gorky I). Aleksandr conducted a stubborn defence of the battery even after it was disabled and he was able to escape after most of the garrison surrendered via an underground drainage duct. He and five other gunners attempted to flee eastwards but were captured on 26 June. After being interrogated, Aleksandr was shot by the SS. Von Manstein later claimed that Aleksandr was 'shot while trying to escape' in order to cover up his culpability in a war crime. (Author's collection)

Once the Soviet flanks began to crumble, von Manstein decided to launch his effort with the 50th and 132nd Infantry Divisions in the centre. The 50th Infantry Division had begun a limited attack with its 121st Infantry Regiment at 0300hrs towards the bridge across the Chernaya River, but at 0505hrs the rest of the division and the adjacent 132nd Infantry Division attacked across the river valley toward Inkerman. The Soviet defences turned out to be rather thin in this area and despite intense mortar fire, the German assault groups were able to cross the valley and fight their way into Inkerman. By 0600hrs, III/123rd Infantry Regiment had made it onto the high ground and captured the Old Fort. The remnants of the 345th Rifle Division collapsed under the German onslaught and LIV Corps was in possession of the Inkerman Heights by noon. Kampfgruppe Walter, formed from the 32nd and 122nd Infantry Regiments, pushed westward to link up with the beachhead. Owing to the lack of effective Soviet response, the Germans had been able to get four regimental *Kampfgruppen* into the bridgehead and had an 8-ton ferry operational by early afternoon. A company of *Panzerjäger* and another of light flak were brought across to strengthen the beachhead. By late afternoon, the 50th Infantry Division spearheads had linked up with the beachhead and several thousand Soviet troops in the vicinity were cut off.

In the south, the day gradually turned into a debacle for the Soviets as the Germans methodically overwhelmed the 386th Rifle Division on Sapun Ridge. As Soviet combat support units started falling back toward Sevastopol, Fretter-Pico committed the 49th Jäger Regiment to pursue the retreating enemy. The *Jäger*, frustrated after weeks of static fighting, took to the pursuit with relish and by nightfall were approaching the English Cemetery on the edge of Sevastopol. During the course of 29 June, XXX Corps took over 2,700 prisoners while LIV Corps had captured about 2,000. German losses for these decisive attacks were only 1,227 casualties, including 135 killed.

ASSAULT CROSSING OF SEVERNAYA BAY BY THE GERMAN LIV CORPS, 0120HRS, 29 JUNE 1942

As the end at Sevastopol approached, von Manstein planned an amphibious finale by General Hansen's LIV Corps to outflank the final Soviet defensive line at Inkerman. Although the Eleventh Army had successfully used this tactic in the Kerch operation, Hansen did not believe it could succeed against an alerted defense. Nevertheless, he began planning a landing operation on the south side of Severnaya Bay near the bombed-out electrical power plant, using two *Kampfgruppen* from the 22nd and 24th Infantry Divisions. The entire divisional artillery of both divisions would support the landing. In order to achieve maximum surprise, the Germans decided not to use an artillery preparation on the opposing shore, but they did use smoke to obscure the embarkation area on the north shore of the bay. A battalion-sized group from the 65th Infantry Regiment and some pioneers under Oberst Schitting boarded 76 assault boats belonging to the 902nd Assault Boat Command after midnight on 29 June and began crossing the 600m-wide stretch of open water. The Germans were taking a terrible risk, since a single Soviet machine-gun position could have wreaked havoc with the flimsy craft, but the Soviets failed to detect the crossing. This area was guarded by the remnants of the 2nd Perekop Regiment and the 79th Naval Infantry Brigade, which occupied trenches atop the dominant hills overlooking the landing area. However, the exhausted units posted to watch the waterfront were unusually lax and the landing was not detected until the first German assault infantry began to engage the pickets.

In this scene, a German platoon from the 65th Infantry Regiment has just landed in six to eight assault boats **(1)** near the power plant **(2)** and has begun to engage a nearby Soviet outpost with MG34s (from the boats)**(3)**, MP40s and stick grenades from the lead troops. The Soviets are just beginning to open fire with a few weapons from nearby buildings and a red flare is fired **(4)** over the nearby hill, indicating that the landing has been spotted. The German Leichtes Sturmboot 39 (light assault boat 39) was a wooden craft that could carry six assault troops at a speed of up to 16 knots. Within 45 minutes of landing, Schitting's assault troops had seized the dominant hills overlooking the beachhead and were pushing inland. The landing was a great success and enabled LIV Corps to strike the strongpoints around Inkerman from behind. By the time that the Soviets began to react to this landing, the Germans had managed to reinforce the beachhead with the four infantry *Kampfgruppen* and some *Panzerjäger* from the 22nd and 24th Infantry Divisions.

A fresh Soviet infantry unit moves up to the front under the cover of cliffs along the edge of Severnaya Bay. Soviet units were most vulnerable when moving into the line, when they were outside their trenches and bunkers. (Central Museum of the Armed Forces, Moscow)

Many Soviet troops were cut off by the sudden German capture of the Sapun Ridge and Inkerman Heights and they made desperate efforts to escape toward Sevastopol before the Germans had thoroughly mopped up these areas. Senior Lieutenant Viktor Ratschkovsky, a Russian artillery battery commander, left his bunker positions near Inkerman with 60 of his troops around 2000hrs on 29 June and attempted to exfiltrate through the Kelin Ravine, but they were surrounded by a German reconnaissance unit and forced to surrender. The staff of the 25th Rifle Division was cut off in the cellar of the champagne factory in Inkerman, where the 47th Medical Battalion had set up a field hospital for about 2,000 wounded soldiers. The commander of the 3rd Naval Infantry Regiment, Podpolkovnik Gussarov, ordered the 150–200 remaining able-bodied sailors to leave the cellar and escape towards Soviet lines once it became dark, but he apparently decided that neither the wounded nor the stockpile of ammunition in the cellar should fall into German hands. At 0120hrs on 30 June nearby German troops witnessed a massive explosion at the champagne factory. As the fall of Sevastopol began to appear imminent, the Soviet leadership became more suicidal and callous towards their own troops.

THE FALL OF SEVASTOPOL, 30 JUNE–4 JULY 1942

By the morning of 30 June, it was obvious to both sides that Sevastopol's defences had been hopelessly compromised by the loss of the Sapun Ridge and the German beachhead on the south side of Severnaya Bay. Aside from the loss of this key terrain, the only large Soviet unit with any remaining combat effectiveness was General-Major Novikov's 109th Rifle Division on the southern coast and the newly arrived 142nd Naval Rifle Brigade. All other units were reduced to battalion-sized or less battlegroups. Even worse, the rapid loss of the area around Inkerman and behind the Sapun Ridge resulted in the loss of all the forward supply dumps and the defenders were now critically short of ammunition. At 0950hrs, the Soviet Stavka ordered the evacuation of Sevastopol and Stalin personally directed the senior military and political leaders to leave the city before it fell.

ABOVE
The remains of Coastal Battery 2, near the North Fort. This position mounted four 100mm guns in open mounts and although protected by the nearby anti-aircraft position at Battery Lenin, it suffered heavy damage from Stuka attacks. Soviet gunners blew up the remaining guns on 20 June and retreated south to the bay. (Nik Cornish Archive, WH685)

ABOVE RIGHT
Von Manstein's secret weapons were the 902nd and 905th Assault Boat Commands, which had over 100 wooden light assault boats. These boats could carry six assault troops and could quickly cross narrow water obstacles such as Severnaya Bay. (Nik Cornish Archive, WH856)

Petrov later wrote that, 'Panic is spreading, particularly among the officers' and news of the evacuation order quickly turned a heretofore-organized defence into a chaotic, 'every-man-for-himself' situation. Fretter-Pico's XXX Corps launched an attack eastwards from the Sapun Ridge with the 28th Light Division and the 170th Infantry Division and found that the Soviets were melting away toward the imagined safety of the Chersonese Peninsula. In short order, the 49th Jäger Regiment advanced almost 6km eastward, capturing the town of Nikolaevka while two regimental *Kampfgruppen* from the 170th Infantry Division swung southwards to take the 109th Rifle Division from behind. The Romanian 1st Mountain Division was also brought in to flank Balaklava's defences. Seeing that he was about to be pinned against the southern coast, Novikov abandoned Balaklava and withdrew 7km westwards to the area around Cape Fiolent.

Around Sevastopol itself, the 28th Light Division's other regiment captured the English Cemetery, and pushed northward to the city outskirts. Hansen's LIV Corps, feeling the effects of three weeks' sustained combat, pushed into the eastern suburbs of Sevastopol known as Korabelnaya, but was content to finish mopping up the last Soviet survivors around Inkerman before pushing into the city. Total German casualties on 30 June were about 821, including 161 killed. At least 4,875 Soviet troops were taken prisoner that day.

By late on 30 June, the Coastal Army held a tenuous line from Cape Fiolent to Sevastopol with the equivalent of only five battalions of infantry. Desperately, a few transport planes were able to land 12 tons of ammunition and less than one ton of food at Chersonese airstrip. At 2000hrs, a meeting of the Military Council of the Black Sea Fleet was held in a casemate at Coastal Battery 35 (Fort Maxim Gorky II to the Germans) in which the decision was made to immediately evacuate the command cadre. Apparently, Petrov and Oktyabrsky gave little thought to saving any of the 23,000 Soviet wounded sheltering in the nearby underground bunkers around Coastal Battery 35. At 0300hrs on 1 July, the submarine *Shch-209* arrived at a dock near Coastal Battery 35 and embarked General-Major Petrov and most of the other senior army leaders from the Coastal Army. As he departed, Petrov ordered General-Major Novikov to take over command of the remnants of the Coastal Army.

On the morning of 1 July, LIV Corps began advancing into the burning ruins of Sevastopol against negligible resistance with the 42nd and 72nd

Infantry Regiments in the lead. A *Kampfgruppe* from the 24th Infantry Division easily captured the anti-aircraft position at the famous Malakhov Hill, then the elusive armoured train 'Zhelezniakov' in a tunnel in Korabelnaya. At 1313hrs, troops from the 72nd Infantry Regiment raised a German flag on the burnt wreckage of the Panorama Museum in southern Sevastopol. Soviet troops inside the city began surrendering in droves, allowing the 72nd Infantry Regiment to reach Artillery Bay by 1400hrs. Sevastopol had fallen and Hansen wasted no time in naming the 42nd Infantry Regiment's commander – Oberst Ernst Maisel – as the new commandant of the city. Von Manstein attempted to exclude the Romanians from participating in the final attack into Sevastopol, but General-maior Gheorghe Manoliu, commander of the Romanian 4th Mountain Division, ignored these orders and sent his troops to raise a Romanian flag on the Nakhimov Monument in the city.

As Sevastopol fell, XXX Corps continued to press the remnants of the Soviet Coastal Army back into the narrow confines of the Chersonese Peninsula. Amazingly, the remnants of the 386th and 388th Rifle Divisions mounted a desperate counterattack against the German 170th Infantry Division and inflicted almost 600 casualties upon XXX Corps. Nevertheless, another 12,600 Soviet troops surrendered on 1 July and organized resistance was approaching an end. Once night fell, 13 transport planes from the Caucasus landed at the Cape Chersonese airstrip and flew out Vice-Admiral Oktyabrsky and 221 members of his staff. With little ado, Petrov, Oktyabrsky and the senior Communist Party leaders had abandoned their brave garrison to its fate.

Shortly after Oktyabrsky departed, the commander of Coastal Battery 35, Captain A. J. Leshchenko, fired his last remaining 305mm rounds at the approaching German forces. Then Leshchenko ordered the detonation of the remaining powder in the magazines, which destroyed both turrets early on 2 July. At 0300hrs, Leshchenko and his gunners ran down to the shore and swam out to a nearby small boat. Although Novikov had been told that no more ships or planes would be sent to evacuate the garrison, a stream of small craft did continue to arrive every night to try and save those who could swim out to them. Novikov himself attempted to flee on a small patrol craft, but was caught.

The final Soviet resistance in the Crimea was offered by the remnants of the 109th Rifle Division fighting from some of the bunkers around Coastal Battery 35, as well as the final defence of the Cape Chersonese airstrip, which fell on 4 July. Although the Soviets made claims that resistance continued for another six to 10 days and that many of the garrison escaped to become partisans in the hills near Yalta, this is simply not true. By evening on 4 July, the Coastal Army was destroyed and the German Eleventh Army had conquered Sevastopol.

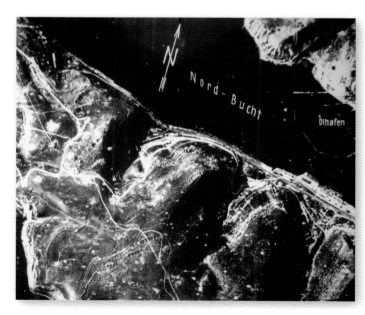

German aerial photo of the area where the 22nd and 24th Infantry Divisions conducted an assault crossing of Severnaya Bay in the pre-dawn hours of 29 June 1942. (NARA)

AFTERMATH

The siege of Sevastopol was a costly battle for both sides. Petrov's Independent Coastal Army was annihilated and of the approximately 118,000 Soviet Army and Navy troops who served in the SOR in June 1942 about 95,000 were captured when the city fell and 5,000 wounded were evacuated. This means that about 18,000 died in the final battle. Seven rifle divisions and six naval rifle brigades were permanently removed from the Soviet order of battle. At least one-third of the Soviet prisoners were wounded. Losses among Sevastopol's civilian population were severe.

Nor had victory been cheap for the Eleventh Army. Total German casualties were at least 4,264 killed, 21,626 wounded and 1,522 missing for a total of over 27,000 casualties. The Romanian units suffered another 8,454 casualties (1,597 killed, 6,571 wounded and 277 missing) for a total Axis loss of 35,866. All of the German infantry divisions required a rest and refit period to recover from a month of sustained close combat and their front-line strength was marginal by the end of the battle. The 22nd and 24th Infantry Divisions had each suffered between 20 and 30 per cent personnel losses, primarily in their infantry battalions. By the end of the battle, the Eleventh Army was essentially incapable of further offensive operations. Its material losses were also substantial with 78 artillery pieces destroyed. During Operation *Störfang*, the Eleventh Army fired off 46,486 tons of ammunition, including 410,000 105mm rounds, 100,000 150mm rounds and over 32,000 *Nebelwerfer* rockets.

Changes in German divisional combat strengths, June–July 1942						
Unit	Battle strength, 1 June 1942	Battle strength, 1 July 1942	Killed	Wounded	Missing	Total losses
22nd Infantry Division	13,445	9,297	670	3,251	395	4,316
24th Infantry Division	11,148	8,811	704	3,295	136	4,135
50th Infantry Division	NA	NA	488	2,784	178	3,450
132nd Infantry Division	9,842	NA	471	2,404	292	3,167
170th Infantry Division	NA	NA	251	1,344	98	1,693

A German truck entering the devastated ruins of Sevastopol in July 1942. Eight months of attacks by enemy bombers and artillery had reduced the city to rubble. (HITM Photo Research)

Before the victory was even complete, von Manstein was promoted to field marshal on 1 July and on 5 July a victory parade was held in the city. While von Manstein departed for a lengthy vacation in Romania, SS-Einsatzgruppe D, moved into Sevastopol and began to dispose of both Jews and Soviet prisoners of war; murdered victims were dumped in the anti-tank ditches outside the city. Once the captured garrison was either murdered, starved or packed off, the SS men turned their attention to the remaining civil population, using mobile vans dubbed 'Soul Killers' to gas their victims. Von Manstein's triumph unleashed a two-year killing spree in the conquered Crimea. Sevastopol itself was put under the thumb of SS-Gruppenführer Ludolf von Alvensleben, an SS police official.

The Germans held Sevastopol for less than two years. In May 1944, the advancing Soviet armies re-entered the Crimea and trapped five German divisions at Sevastopol. Soviet assault troops stormed the Sapun Ridge on 7/8 May 1944 and the defeated Axis troops fled to the Chersonese Peninsula, where the Coastal Army had been crushed 22 months prior. On 12 May 1944, the last Axis resistance on the Chersonese Peninsula was crushed. Although the Axis managed to evacuate about half the Seventeenth Army, some 31,700 German and 25,800 Romanian troops were killed or captured at Sevastopol. Soviet troops found that Sevastopol was virtually destroyed after two sieges.

As the end of the war approached, Sevastopol was proclaimed a 'Hero City' by order of Stalin on 1 May 1945. Soviet postwar historians and the Party attempted to mythologize the siege of Sevastopol by creating heroes and downplaying the fact that its military and political leaders had abandoned the garrison.

THE BATTLEFIELD TODAY

Only five to ten buildings in Sevastopol survived World War II, so the city had to be completely rebuilt. Unlike other demolished Soviet cities, Sevastopol received considerable resources for reconstruction so once again it could serve as the main headquarters of the Black Sea Fleet. However, the beginning of the Cold War resulted in Sevastopol being closed to foreigners for almost four decades and it was not until 1996 that these restrictions began to ease. Sevastopol's status began to change with the break up of the Soviet Union in 1991 and the independence of the Ukraine. Eventually, Russia divided the Black Sea Fleet with Ukraine and it maintains a lease on the naval base until 2019.

Sevastopol's postwar reconstruction also included the extraordinary step of rebuilding Coastal Battery 30 with two triple 305mm gun turrets from the scrapped battleship *Poltava*. Work began on the coastal battery in 1947 and was completed in 1954; the battery was once again operational and remained so until the 1990s. Today, the two turrets still sit atop the same ridge south of the Belbek River Valley, although much of this area still belongs to the Russian military and is off limits. Indeed, much of the area north of Severnaya Bay has changed considerably from 1942 in that most of the wartime forts and bunker positions have given way to urban housing areas and new roads. Sites such as Fort Stalin are now merely tree-covered hills, with only a few concrete reminders of the war visible.

Inside Sevastopol, the Museum of the Black Sea Fleet has two exhibit halls devoted to telling the story of the fleet in World War II. The Malakhov Hill, although primarily concerned with the heroic defence of Sevastopol in the 1854–55 siege, also has some displays relating to World War II. Outside the museum there is a monument to the Soviet fighter pilots who defended the city, topped by a model of a Yak-1 fighter.

The main World War II memorial for Sevastopol is a large diorama and museum located just south of the Serpentine atop the Sapun Heights outside the city. However, this museum was established during the Communist era and was intended to celebrate the city's liberation by the Red Army in 1944, not its defence in 1941–42. The main museum is located in a U-shaped diorama building, entitled 'Storm of Sapun Mountain'. Nearby, there is an exhibit of World War II Soviet artillery, tanks and naval equipment. However, most of these weapons displayed were not used in the 1942 siege of Sevastopol. Very little German equipment is displayed, but there is a 50mm Pak 38 anti-tank gun and a 105mm l.FH 18 howitzer that are posted in reconstructed firing positions. While visitors may not actually learn much

about the events of 1941–42 from this over-the-top display, the terrain is still much like it was in 1942 and this area is still largely undeveloped.

Proceeding farther south to Balaklava, visitors can find some examples of World War II bunkers and trench systems still in existence. Near the southeast entrance into Balaklava Bay, there are the ancient ruins of the Genoese Cembalo fortress, which is open to tourists. This rocky and barren terrain, known as the 'Sulzbacher' to the Germans, blocked their entrance into Balaklava along the coast. On the Chersonese Peninsula, the remains of Coastal Battery 35 are still accessible, but the Soviets chose not to rebuild this battery. Sevastopol still suffers from unexploded ordinance since the area was under constant attack for over eight months; in February 2004 a 900kg German airdropped magnetic mine was found by scrap hunters in Kazachiya Bay and it exploded, killing three men.

After liberation, Sevastopol's embittered citizens refused to bury German war dead and many were eventually sent back to Germany. However, in 1998 a German military cemetery was opened in the village of Goncharnoye near Sevastopol and now has over 11,000 German soldiers interred there.

German troops investigate the remains of Turret No. 2 of Coastal Battery 30 after the battle. This turret was knocked out by a glancing blow from a 600mm concrete-piercing shell from one of the Karl mortars on 6 June 1942. The mortar round tore off a slab of armour from the turret roof, which lies atop the 305mm barrel on the left. (Nik Cornish Archive, WH670)

BIBLIOGRAPHY

PRIMARY SOURCES
German Records at NARA: Eleventh Army; XXX and LIV Corps; 22nd, 24th, 50th, 72nd, 132nd, 170th Infantry Divisions, 28th Light Division

OTHER SOURCES
Krasnoznamennyi Chernomorskoi flot Moscow: Voenizdat, 1987

'Oborona 79-I strelkovoi brigady pod Sevastopolem v iune 1942' in *Sbornik voenno-istoricheskikh materialov Velikoi Otechestvennoi voine* Moscow: Voenizdat, 1954

'Sturm auf Sevastopol' *Signal*, Nr. 16, II August 1942, pp. 12–17

Achkasov V. I., and Pavlovich N. B., *Soviet Naval Operations in the Great Patriotic War 1941–45* Annapolis, MD: Naval Institute Press, 1981

Bergström, Christer, and Mikhailov, Andrey, *Black Cross/Red Star, Volume 2* Pacifica, California: Pacifica Military History, 2001

Egger, Martin, *Die Festung Sewastopol. Dokumentation ihrer Befestigungsanlagen und der Kämpfe 1942* Cologne: Harry Lippman, 1995

Hayward, Joel, 'A Case Study in Early Joint Warfare: An Analysis of the Wehrmacht's Crimean Campaign of 1942' in *The Journal of Strategic Studies*, Vol. 22, No. 4 (December 1999), pp. 103–130.

Hayward, Joel S., *Stopped at Stalingrad* Lawrence, KS: University Press of Kansas, 1998)

Ignatovic, E. A., *Zenitnoe bratstvo Sevastopolya* Kiev: izdatelstvo politiceskoy literatury, 1986

Karpov, Vladimir V., *Commander* London: Brassey's, 1987

Krylov, Nikolai I., *Ne Pomerknet Nikogda* Moscow: Military Publishing, 1984

Kurowski, Franz, *Sewastopol. Der Angriff auf die stärkste Festung der Welt 1942* Friedberg: Podzun-Pallas, 2002

Manstein, Erich von, *Lost Victories* Novato, CA: Presidio Press, 1986

Perecnev, H., and Vinogradov, H., *Na strazhe morskikh gorizontov* Moscow: Soviet Ministry of Defence, 1967

Rohwer, Jurgen, *Chronology of the War at Sea 1939–1945* London: Chatham Publishing, 2005)

Rosselli, Alberto, 'Activities of the Italian MAS and Pocket Submarines in the Black Sea: 1942–1943' on www.regiamarina.net site

Sweeting, C. G., *Blood and Iron: The German Conquest of Sevastopol* Washington, DC: Brassey's Inc., 2004

Wernet, Dieter and Inge, 'Maksim Gorky I: A Recent Example of the Re-use of Naval Turrets in Coast Defenses' *Warship International*, No. 1, 1997

Winkel, Walte , *Der Kampf Um Sewastopol* Berg am see: Kurt Vowinckel Verlag, 1984

INDEX

References to illustrations are shown in **bold**.